Cornwall and Devon

70 years of volunteering
for military service 1846 to 1916

Everett Sharp

authorHOUSE

AuthorHouse™ UK
1663 Liberty Drive
Bloomington, IN 47403 USA
www.authorhouse.co.uk
Phone: UK TFN: 0800 0148641 (Toll Free inside the UK)
UK Local: (02) 0369 56322 (+44 20 3695 6322 from outside the UK)

Published by AuthorHouse   09/21/2022

ISBN: 978-1-7283-7555-7 (sc)
ISBN: 978-1-7283-7554-0 (e)

Print information available on the last page.

CONTENTS

With grateful thanks to my family whose eyes glaze over when I mention WW1.
Friends and good neighbours, ditto.
My son Christopher – many, many thanks for your technical expertise.
A very special thank you to my wife Judith, 50 years married,
still tolerating my discourses and being the
best editor, in more ways than one, ever.

INTRODUCTION

This book answers the question - did the people of Cornwall and Devon differ in their reactions to the declaration of war in August 1914 up to the introduction of conscription in 1916 from elsewhere in the UK?

As a background to that question I also look at any previous popularity of volunteering for part-time military service, firstly in the Government funded Militia and Yeomanry and the initially civilian controlled 'Rifles'. This is followed by the service of these volunteers in the Second Boer War and recruiting for the new Territorial Force established in 1907. I have also included details of the so-called 1846 'invasion scares' and discuss the possibly influential growth of invasion fiction.

180 years ago both counties were isolated from the mainstream, the far West Penwith in Cornwall being reached quicker and easier by boat than road travel but even this being precarious because of the dangerous shoals, reefs and the pernicious sea itself. Today, with the ever growing possibility of the partial or possibly permanent separation of the 'British isles' into its constituent parts, were there even then nuanced attitudes and a different or localised patriotism in times of national distress?

As I do not wish to merely rehash what has been written before I have undertaken original research by using newspapers printed during this period and available to read using https://www.britishnewspaperarchive.co.uk/ that for a small fee allows you on-line access. Each newspaper is named and its text is verbatim but shown in italics, one thing to be aware of, it surprised me that on many occasions the spelling and punctuation are poor. Any required explanations added are in normal script. Using this I will investigate how much were the people of the two West Country counties told about what was going on in the greater outside world, how much did they care, or what did they care about? We will see what was published and did this represent a fair judgement or did it lean towards pure propaganda?

I have also used many of the books concerning the period in my collection and all of these, or articles to which I do refer, will be identified by author, title, date and page number at the rear of the book.

I have also used many of the books concerning the period in my collection and all of these, or articles to which I do refer, will be identified by author, title, date and where possible, the page number.

CHAPTER ONE

A History of Volunteering

This chapter deals in part with the types of volunteer and early militia units as outlined below, indicating the military nature of the state's relationship with its subjects as bodies of trained men up to 1914. It was after that year when large numbers of women became a valued and integral part of the armed forces during the Great War until today.

Over the next pages I will initially consider in some depth the government funded militia followed by the independent Volunteer Rifle and Artillery Movement and finally I will touch upon the volunteer Yeomanry cavalry.

Before I go on to discuss these subjects, we need know the approximate number of people who were able to read a newspaper, i.e., those who may have been influenced to volunteer, or had an interest outside of their own family, household, street, hamlet, village or town.

In 1840 adult male literacy grew from around 70 percent and increased by 10 percent every 20 years. For women, although this has a lower starting rate at 60 percent it experienced a sharper increase until both reached 100 percent by the turn of the century[1].

These figures are disputed, even as to the effect of Forster's Education Act of 1870. A.N Wilson, in his *magnum opus* 'The Victorians', is rather scathing of the idea that British people needed state interference to give them the ability to read and write. Using a series of statistics, he states that 79 percent of Northumberland miners and 87 percent of East Anglian workhouse reared children were literate in the 1830s[2]. However, in its support Tabatha Jackson writes that the effect of the Act increased literacy from 63.3 percent in 1841 to 92.2 percent in 1900[3]. Whatever the statistics, between 1846 and 1916 most of the adult population were able to read and write.

Militia

Before 1660 county militias were the chief means of defending the kingdom, its men were liable for both home service and serving abroad. The origins of these locally raised, conscripted units goes back about 1,000 years to the arrangements made by Alfred the Great (872 - 901) to combat the threat posed by Viking invasions. Obviously the rules, laws, and regulations changed radically over subsequent centuries reacting to both internal and external threats.

In the 18th century the government recognised significant weaknesses in the then system. Consequently the 1757 Militia Act and 1802 Militia Act plus other legislation, changed the regulations so reforming the basis on which men could be levied in time of need and their length of service[4]. One of the most significant being that the militia would not be required to serve abroad; they were only to serve within the British Isles.

If the counties could not meet their allocated quota of men aged between 18 and 45 they filled their ranks by means of conscription with all names being drawn by ballot from lists of those males deemed able-bodied, as happened to Devon in 1640[5]. Initially, if affluent, those chosen could pay a bounty to a delegated substitute who would serve in their place. In 1802 the definition of able-bodied was refined, mainly in an attempt to prevent the poorest being called up and therefore leaving their families as a burden on the parish. The numbers required were strictly monitored and adhered to with every parish penalised if they did not supply the required number of men. Those who fell short sought volunteers and paid them a bounty to serve[6].

As stated, to ensure home defence the militia could not fight overseas. However, for those willing to join the army there was a carefully monitored system allowing for individual militiamen to volunteer after three years service, later extended to five.

In 1815 after the defeat of Napoleon and with the consequent lack of an invasion threat, the ballot system was done away with. In fact the numbers of militiamen were greatly reduced to save money. This Georgian 'peace dividend' then led to torpor and in 1831, the home defence militias were disbanded or to use the legal term 'disembodied'.

This continued for fourteen years until 1845 when the government *'partially conceded to the desire expressed by the country for re-embodiment'*[7] and pressure from Lord Wellington and Sir John Burgoyne [see below]. What was expected of these 'new' volunteers? Unfortunately, correct or not, the attitude of the general Victorian populace to the militia was a very poor one and had evolved little from those of the seventeenth and early eighteenth centuries - for example Jane Austen's 'Cad' George Wickham from her 1813 novel *Pride and Prejudice* - or soldiers in general as in the earlier Mary Wollstonecraft's *A Vindication of the Rights of Women* (1792). Also, the attitudes of the newspapers of 1840s, although playing a role in wanting a revival of the militia, were so obviously condescending. They started labelling the Militia as four main types: corpulent old gentlemen, foppish young officers, social climbers from the middling sorts and ragged lower ranks. Attitudes that obviously did not help the force recruit from the respectable working classes as had been hoped when re-established. Other factors were also to blame, two being[8] the role of the military in suppressing popular disturbances in the early nineteenth century and the lack of funding even to the provision of decent uniforms.

The government had also bowed to pressure brought about because of the new and varied invasion scares that disturbed the early Victorians' peace of mind. The Industrial Revolution had quickly ushered in new technology such as rifles, trains and iron hulled boats. Although there were no planes at the time there were plenty of popular look-into-the-future publications with fantastic flying machines. As early as the 1840s, to capitalise on this concern both for financial gain and societal change magazine articles were 'forewarning' that, in the near future, enemy balloons would be wreaking destruction[9].

Seemingly these articles and a story in the press did push the establishment to at least examine the problem and ask if a change was needed in policy. In the mid 1840s they reported that Lord Wellington, the Commander in Chief of the British Army, had written two memoranda, both expressing concerns about the vulnerability of English naval dockyards to an attack by the French[10]. Disturbing indeed to read the phrase *'we are not safe for a week after the declaration of war'* [by the French and Americans] that had been leaked to the press, contained within a letter from Wellington to the Inspector General of Fortifications, Sir John Burgoyne[11].

At this time the French had begun construction of the world's first ironclad fleet that, combined with better steam engines, the screw propeller, rifled ordnance and armour plate, made them a powerful potential enemy as obviously the superiority of our 'wooden walls' - i.e., the ships of the Royal Navy - was now challenged, even superseded. It can be seen that any supposed superiority was negated because of the technological advances in the first few decades of the nineteenth century[12].

However, not everyone was fearful. Britain was undergoing great change and with the stirrings of the Industrial Revolution the potential for great profit became ever more widespread. War eats men and gold and is not conducive to stability or trading. Free Trade was advocated by Britain's brilliant, radical Whig politician Richard Cobden, a self-made and, for the age, a very well travelled man. He campaigned strongly against the theory that for British safety you must have a balance of power with other major nations to guarantee the peace. This attitude, he stated, actually made nations distrustful or worried, thus reducing the ability to deal financially with them to the advantage of both, especially Britain.

The battle for both the minds and the purses of the public began to be waged in the newspapers. The following is a copy of a letter addressed by the Duke of Wellington to Sir John Burgoyne:

Exeter and Plymouth Gazette - Saturday 8th January 1848
THE NATIONAL DEFENCES. A previous letter, it was said had been written by the Duke of Wellington to Sir John Burgoyne on the important subject of the defence of the Country from Foreign Invasion. ....It may be upon that the surest way to maintain peace is to be fully prepared for war. We gain far more from our fears than their love.

Possibly in a way of trying to gain some sort of balance and to lessen readers' worries the Gazette adds an article from the satirical magazine Punch. This advocated the idea of *'placing fire-engines on cliff tops to play liberally an invading army with chloroform, to reduce the whole host to a state of utter insensibility'*.

Weekly Dispatch (London) - Sunday 9th January 1848
But as we stand now, and if it be true that the exertions of the fleet alone are not sufficient to provide for our defence, we are not safe for a week after the declaration of war.

What of the opposition to this idea and Wellington's militant and military stance?

The West Country had long been a Whig and then Liberal stronghold, consequently at least one rebuttal was published, a letter from Cobden confirming his support for Joseph Sturge, a Quaker and peace and anti-slavery campaigner who had called a meeting:

North Devon Journal - Thursday 27th January 1848
THE NATIONAL DEFENCES. At preliminary meeting held on the 10th inst., with a view convening a public meeting in the Town-hall, Birmingham, to consider the propriety of petitioning Parliament against the anticipated increase in the national defences and the enrolment of the militia…..

"My dear Sturge, Pencarrow, near Bodmin. (Cornwall) Jan 12th

To me it utterly unintelligible why we should now be suddenly stunned with this outcry for additional armaments to protect us against attack….."

Their points of view did not win the argument, especially the suspicions raised just three years later after the seizure of power in France by another Bonaparte, Louis Napoleon the Third with the help of the army[13]. This caused one of the 'Three Panics' outlined by Cobden. The first of 1846-47, then 1851-52 and finally 1858-59 which initially came about, as we have seen above, by the French threatening the superiority of the Royal Navy with the construction of the world's first 'ironclad' fleet[13]. The Royal Navy, playing catch-up, launched its first 'Ironclad', HMS Warrior in December 1860; see Angus Konstam *'British Ironclads 1860 -75'* Osprey Publications.

This was not the first increase in military spending however, as previously to this the British Government had also recognised that 'something had to be done' for the army. It subsequently passed the 1852 Militia Bill that allowed for 80,000 militia men and 3,000 extra regulars. However, showing restraint, Parliament decided not to reintroduce the compulsory ballot 'stick', with the proviso that this could be to be resorted to in time of war to fill the ranks, instead relying on the 'carrot' of a financial bounty.

Robert Slaney MP is recorded in Hansard as stating *"he was glad that the Government had determined to raise this body of men by bounty, and not by the ballot. The former, he thought, was the only just and right way in which to raise a force. It was not fair to compel the humbler classes to pay as much for providing a substitute as would have to be paid by the rich*[14].

There were worries concerning the so called Revolutions of 1848 spreading to the discontented in this country and especially Ireland. Also included were the Chartists who were asking, rather politely considering the bloodshed on the Continent, with a petition for voting reform.

But they were also sensationally reported as entertaining so called Irish 'rebels' who were enjoying the 'London season' according to the news.

However, one newspaper sought to reassure its upper and middle class readers that there was nothing for them to fear:

Manchester Times - Tuesday 01 August 1848
The continent is a prey to intestine disorders and neither willing nor able to stir a finger against us. We have at least 50,000 disciplined men, the finest troops in the world, in Ireland a large fleet on the coast and the most experienced and skilful officers of the day to command them.

For all this papers bellicosity the establishment was concerned. Hence there was near certainty in granting more money for the armed services.

Royal Cornwall Gazette - Friday 16th April 1852
The government Militia Bill, ….. to consolidate and amend the laws relating to the militia in England, has been printed. There are 32 sections. It is declared to be expedient, "for better fulfilling the purposes of the institution of the militia with as little disturbance as may be to the ordinary occupations of the people, that the laws for raising and regulating the militia should be amended.

Royal Cornwall Gazette - Friday 20th August 1852
ARMY and NAVY. Rifle Muskets.— The Commander-in-Chief desires that the rifle muskets now in the course of supply to the troops, which it is proposed shall in the first instance be furnished at the rate of 100 stand for each regiment, and the arming of the recent augmentation of the infantry thereby be provided for, may be distributed in equal numbers among the companies of each regiment and depot, and placed in the hands of the best and most experienced marksmen.

It was now that Devon led the way with the a new locally funded 'militia' that was independent of central Government control, the local and volunteer Exeter and South Devon Rifles a year later in 1853. This initial patriotic 'seed' grew to affect the whole of the UK, see below.

By this time enlistment in the militia had become more acceptable in all classes for various reasons, not all patriotic. At best it took working men with menial boring employment and gave them a pride, more money and the feeling of comradeship as they possibly fulfilled Dr Johnson's thoughts about carrying a musket; but we must also acknowledge that many of the public thought that the extra money would be, and unfortunately was, spent on alcohol to an excessive degree.

At a time of an expanding empire, for the upper and middle classes, much more importantly there was a chance to show leadership. Thus they could exhibit to all what they thought of as their proper place in society, with an added bonus that it gave a potential officer a 'toe in the water' the chance to see if the military life suited them[15].

The Militia began to be celebrated:

Royal Cornwall Gazette - Friday 6th January 1860
During dinner, the band of the Royal Cornwall Miners' Artillery Militia was stationed in the gallery, and played a number of airs and selections from some of the operas; and at the conclusion of the repast the ladies were admitted into the gallery.

Cornish Times - Saturday 28th April 1866
Cornish Militia Regiments. One hundred recruits of the Royal Cornwall Rangers' Militia, under the command of Capt. and Adjutant Alms and Lieut. Gilbert (musketry instructor), have assembled at Bodmin tor a week's preparatory training. About 50 recruits of the Royal Cornwall and Devon Miners Artillery Militia have assembled at Pendennis Castle for preliminary drill on Wednesday just, but more are expected.

The paper then goes on to report the country wide strength of the militia:-

The establishment of the militia regiments of the United Kingdom consisted last year of 4686 officers, 5,027, non-commissioned officers, with 124,622 privates. There were present training on the day of inspection 2,407 Officers, 4,509 non-commissioned officers, and 85,850 privates. There were absent from training on the same day, 449 officers with leave, 25 officers without leave, 52 non-commissioned officers with leave, six non-commissioned officers without leave, 1,810 privates with leave, and 6.719 privates without leave. There were 'wanting to complete' 1,734 officers, 474 non-commissioned officers, and 30,307 privates. The large number of privates 'wanting to complete' is stated to have been chiefly caused by the reduction made in August, 1861, in the effective strength in all regiments whose establishments exceed privates.

By 1871 with the abolition of the purchase of a commission in the regular army a further inducement came the way of those who wanted to take the 'toe in the water' of earlier years [above] a leap forward. A commission in the militia did not require a young man to attend the British Army officer training establishment at Sandhurst. After which, if he passed an examination he could transfer into regular service. At a later date two future field marshals, John French and Henry Wilson, both gained their regular commissions this way[16].

Throughout the country because this could also be seen as the gathering of those with a higher social standing all at most gatherings officers were named:

Express and Echo - Monday 1st June 1874
The old hands of the lst Devon Militia assembled to-day at the Depot, St. Thomas. The muster was as follows This comprised the rank and name of 15 officers plus *Drum Major G. James, 18 bandsmen 10 Sergeants, 497 rank and file. Three were absent 6 officers, stick and temporary leave, men, 67 men without leave, and 25 accounted for. The regiment left the depot at five by march route for Dawlish.*

As usual in Britain social standing mattered and snobbery abounded, I suspect that many Lord Lieutenants of the County would have subscribed to the 'clever' or snide saying that "a greengrocer with a volunteer commission was not an officer but a greengrocer pleased".

It was, however, recognised that home grown enthusiasm had to be replaced by a more professional amalgamation with the regular forces and consequently, seven years later in 1881 came great change. The new amalgamations creating infantry regiments consisting of two battalions also changed the status of the militia making them the 3rd Battalion.

Further reforms followed in 1908 swept away the county's militias' who now had to adopt the title the Special Reserve [see below]. In fact this battalion became an administrative and training unit never leaving the British Isles, with the duty of providing trained recruits in time of war.

As it never saw military action it would be too easy to think of it as an anachronism but this does not do the volunteer militia justice. They had proved their worth by being an available source of manpower to be called upon in times of military crisis and therefore to be recognised as part of Britain's defences by any potential enemy.

The Volunteer Rifles and Artillery.

As we have seen above the threat of invasion after 1815 brought about a radical reduction of part time volunteers paid and equipped by the government and finally in 1831 its 'disembodiment'. However, with the French regaining their military strength once again and the perceived threat of an enemy landing on our shores and conquering the country loomed large with certain sections of the community. Consequently the 1850s were in turmoil, a whirligig of pacifists versus militants versus politicians versus militia and all, versus some, but not all of the army. This stirred by an ever increasing diet of invasion literature [see below] plus French and later German military thoughts on the subject being published in the press.

In reaction to a perceived threat the educated and growing middle class began forming both mounted and dismounted voluntary rifle and artillery companies' independent of government funding. As we have seen Exeter had led the way as early as 1853[17], then Liverpool in 1859 both starting out as uncoordinated units. These were initially not welcomed by the Prime Minister, Lord Derby's first ministry, or members of Parliament and many senior army officers. Not only were they seen as part-time 'amateur soldiers' but also that they could interfere with recruitment to the regular army[18], with the Commander-in-Chief, the very conservative and anti-reformist Duke of Cambridge referring to them as a 'dangerous rabble'.

However, because of the parliamentary pressure these groups could bring, by the time of Derby's second ministry in 1859 they were legally recognised as the Volunteer Movement. Even so and to express their independence from central authority, they arbitrarily organised themselves into sub-districts, positively distancing themselves from the more, to their eyes, plebeian militia. For example here in the West Country we have this long, but very informative article:

Launceston Weekly News and Cornwall & Devon Advertiser. -
Saturday 28th May 1859
RIFLE CORPS. The daily papers teem with letters and reports of public meetings on this subject A tithe of them would more than fill our columns…. One of the best articles on the subject is the following, which appeared in the Times of Tuesday, signed "A North Riding Volunteer" …….

For this end each private should bring testimonial -of character for honesty and sobriety, either from his clergyman, from deputy-lieutenant, or magistrate of his immediate neighbourhood, or from an officer of the corps into which he wishes to enter….

Firstly, a good rifle; whether a muzzle or breech loader is a matter of serious consideration. The advantages of each are considerable. I lean to the latter for the following reasons it is more rapidly loaded—say as three is to one. It never fails…..

Officers and privates should furnish their own uniforms, that of the officers differing in nothing from that of their men except in superiority of material.

Officers might carry the ordinary military sword Instead of the sword bayonet.

North Devon Journal - Thursday 30th June 1859

The response to the appeal, "Riflemen, form!" appears to have been pretty general throughout the country, least so far public meetings on the subject are concerned, at each of which patriotic fervour found a safety valve. The mania has extended even to Barnstaple, where a committee has been formed to enlist volunteer riflemen. In the prospect of a great national danger, it would become a duty of universal obligation for Englishmen to prepare to defend their altars and their homes, and we are assured that an invading foe would meet with such reception as would make him rue the day that he placed his feet upon our shores…..

The above is suggesting that only men of some means could join such units. The indication is the man must be what used to be called 'a good sort' the type who can provide his own uniform, complete, as the writer goes on to specify the type of overcoat, waist belt and, for Riflemen a short sword. Tradition in the army today still has such named units fixing swords and not bayonets. It is a term left over from the Napoleonic Wars and the then new Baker Rifle being a shorter weapon than the musket, needed the longer 'sword' for defence against cavalry. That volunteer officers should carry a 'regular sword' was to indicate their status and, by extension, a social *cache* that could be seen as possibly one of the reasons for joining.

Looking at other areas of the country of the 45 men enrolled in the proposed Amersham (Buckinghamshire) Corps approximately 54 percent of the identified Volunteers were middle class. In the Winslow sub division of the 3rd Bucks (Buckingham and Winslow) Rifle Volunteer Corps approximately 80 percent of identified volunteers considered themselves of similar social elite. One unit, the 2nd Beds (Toddington) has been researched and only one member not identified. Here the breakdown is 37 percent upper middle class, 35 percent lower middle class and over 21percent artisan class[19] such was the obsessive stratification of society at this time.

Those with authority locally in Cornwall were likewise enthusiastic:

Royal Cornwall Gazette - Friday 2nd December 1859
RIFLE CORPS AT HELSTON. A large and influential meeting was held in the Guildhall at Helston, on Wednesday, 30th November, at noon, convened by the Mayor, to consider the expediency of forming a Rifle Corps for Helston and its neighbourhood, in aid of the National Defences….. he believed all would agree that our National Defences were not on a sound and proper footing. For the past ten years all the great nations of Europe had been increasing their armies, navies, and coast defences, and he dwelt at some length on what had been done by Russia, France, Spain, Prussia, Sweden, and Denmark, and forcibly urged that the time had arrived when England should increase her national defences by the means of a Rifle Corps.

However, the parsimonious decision of the government during the early days of the Rifle movement greatly hampered this idea in Cornwall. The Lord Lieutenant of the County, Lord Vivian, warned The Secretary of State for War, General Jonathan Peel, that although the local people had enough money for their day to day needs they did not possess a surplus to enable them to buy uniforms or weapons, and more significantly, they were disinclined to accept the 'discipline requisite' in military units[20]. Because of the perception of increased external threats changes followed and it must have been pleasing to those of the county wishing to join a local unit this had changed by 1875 [see below].

Western Times - Thursday 15th December 1859
A meeting for the formation of a Rifle Corps was held at Tiverton yesterday. The Mayor, Mr. Gath, presided. The chief speakers were Mr. J. Amory, and Admiral Tucker. The subject was very heartily taken up. Lord and the Hon. Mr. Desman, the members for the borough had both expressed their cordial concurrence it, both being volunteer riflemen in London. Upwards of £100 was subscribed the meeting, and many volunteers enrolled their name in the course of the day. Tiverton will, we have no doubt, take rank among the towns most determined to uphold the national independence the hour of need.

It was not an inexpensive undertaking as pointed out by The Exeter and Plymouth Gazette of Saturday the 17th December 1859 that carried an advertisement stating the cost of one complete set of clothing for a volunteer amounted to £2.25 or 55 shillings. This would be about four weeks wages for a farm labourer or a seaman. Note that at this stage he would also need to buy a rifle at £10 [200 shillings] or about seven weeks wages, plus, as can be imagined, the other requisites such as an overcoat and a stout pair of boots. These charges clearly show the impossibility for such working men to 'aspire' to the volunteers. But for those who could afford such premium costs their social acceptability was obvious.

Such acceptability forced a social rethink as reflected in local newspapers such as the North Devon Journal. Just 11 years before had been against such a movement but had become an enthusiastic supporter, reflecting I suspect the revised attitude of its now 'patriotic' readers, and without a blush of cynicism. Over time the Rifle Volunteers became part of everyday society. They were welcomed as Britain began to worry that the islands should soon be invaded and that this country would have to fight, somebody, even extra terrestrials as described by HG Wells. Sensation sells newspapers and magazines so stories concerning invasion, treachery, as shown in *The Railway Children* and spies living amongst us proliferated.

Such fiction continued to promote great concern that supported and promoted the idea of home grown military units:

Royal Cornwall Gazette - Friday 17th August 1860
INVASION. To the Editor of the Royal Cornwall Gazette.

Sir, I am not far-sighted enough to discover, whether any hostile troops will, during my day, approach the Anglican coasts, but there seems to be indirect evidence to show that "the powers that be" themselves do not forthwith expect an invasion. It is indeed true that two millions of money have been voted for the National Defences to fortify places, if I am rightly in- formed, that are already nearly impregnable ; or ports that are too far up Channel, to be visited in haste, by any judicious opponent in Western Europe. Should any unfriendly armaments be sent from Toulon or Brest, common sense would direct them to the nearest port in the British Channel, where the approaches, at all times of tide, are safe and easy.. .... I cannot learn that the authorities have decided on expending a penny of these millions on Pendennis Castle, which might be made to command the great roadstead, where numerous troops, I fear, could be disembarked without delay.....

The above is an example that this section of the literate Victorian British classes had developed a 'siege mentality' or that feeling of insecurity based possibly on 'the more you have, the more you have to worry about losing it'. This was exacerbated in part by a dramatic change some 11 years later when in 1871 came the almighty shock that Prussia, a previously considered Second Rate Power, beat the French so decisively[21] in the Franco-Prussian War. This also resulted in a unified Germany striding onto the world stage as a Great Power. Following the upset and using the defeat as an indication of an imagined 'what could happen' came the most famous of invasion stories the seminal *Battle of Dorking* (1871)[22]. This work of obvious fiction purports to be an account of a German invasion of the United Kingdom and where, cleverly, the author advances change as he supports conscription to be introduced. This argument for universal military service is supported as the invaders conquer because, besides new technology, they have a vast conscript army. These books and events were calculated to awake in some cases, or confirm within the emerging middle class, new anxieties about the future of Europe. They also pointed to more uncertainty when it came to foreign policy. It also produced within elements of the public a growing objection to treasury limits concerning the army. They also found troubling subsequent government's resistance to conscription or policies that allowed little increase in the militia. Hence the growing popularity of the various volunteer Rifle and Artillery units.

Express and Echo - Saturday 19th June 1875
NEWTON ABBOT. The members of the 10th Devon Rifle Volunteer Corps left Newton this morning for the camp at Totnes, where they will remain for eight days.

Tavistock Gazette - Friday 15th October 1875
TAVISTOCK. WEDNESDAY, NOV. 3rd, 1875. MR. T. W. HUSSEY will read Robertson's celebrated comedy of "CASTE." Each character will be personated. The above reading will take place in connection with the 22nd Devon Volunteer Rifle Corps.

In fact Devon again led the way. Here, to increase professionalism within the volunteers Devon introduced a centralised command structure, this becoming the model that other counties subsequently copied.

The Cornish Telegraph - Thursday 26th May 1881
CHURCH PARADE OF THE PENZANCE RIFLE VOLUNTEERS. The (Penzance) Company P.C.R.V. paid annual visit Gulval parish church on Sunday. In the absence Captain Bouse, through indisposition, Lieut. Mathews in command. The company mustered strong—96 of all ranks, and was accompanied by the excellent band, under Mr. Wigg. The weather being delightfully fine, large number accompanied the volunteers, and the church was so crowded that many sat on forma and chairs placed in the aisles.

Cornubian and Redruth Times - Friday 15th July 1881
Friday, July 15, 1881 OUR VOLUNTEER ARMY England has some reason to feel proud of her volunteer army. It is admitted all hands that the success of the great review at Windsor was complete.

Questions, however, continued to emerge within the army as to the various volunteer units' abilities and readiness. This obviously created friction between the well meaning civilians and senior officers with many of the latter looking at the various county associations as not real soldiers, no matter how well turned out they may be. Opposed to this the Rifle Volunteers saw themselves as a middle class 'citizen army'. They were as independently thinking as many of them were financially secure[23], they would do things 'their way' which even included the fact that each member only had to give 14 days' notice to leave. This negated any threat of persecution under the Mutiny Act[24], an attitude that worried even the less scathing in the army; could the majority of riflemen be relied on?

Concerns and the need for guaranteed reliability the movement bowed to pressure as from 1880 increasing government funding also brought greater supervision that led to changes in standards. Firstly, consolidation of the many numbered, into lettered (A,B,C etc.) companies within a Corps, followed by, a year later further reorganisation as the 1ˢᵗ, 2ⁿᵈ,3ʳᵈ etc. Volunteer Battalions of their county regiments. Ultimately the organization was not tested during an invasion of these islands, but a minority did see service in the Second Boer War, [see below].

Even with an increase in perceived external threats, for the regular British Army at this time there was still no Government funding nor of a strong impetuous for introducing conscription. In fact there was resistance to the very idea with an element of mocking '*sang froid*'.

Cornish & Devon Post - Saturday 31ˢᵗ July 1880

…..this worry was expressed and utilized by those wishing to expand the British army by the introduction of, continental style conscription …… till the Russians or somebody else invade India through Afghanistan, a contingency about as probable German invasion of Great Britain through Ireland….

Over time with opinions aired when heightened by perceived increased threat levels or too much liquid refreshment the arguments flared then spluttered on….

The Cornish Telegraph - Thursday 12ᵗʰ March 1885

On the contrary, Sir John St Aubyn has delighted hearers the dear expression of his views upon variety of home topics…. General Hamley commences his article in rather alarmist strain, declaring that in all the years since the beginning of the Volunteer movement there has never been so much reason as now provide against the formidable contingency of an invasion….. the protection of the southern counties he considers that an increase of the local Volunteer force by fifty-two thousand men also necessary.

Cornubian and Redruth Times - Friday 24ᵗʰ April 1885

OUR CITIZEN SOLDIERS. It was not till the fall of the French Empire in 1870 that our military authorities began to be roused from the apathy with which they had long regarded the patriotic movement…..

And with some, you may think, with smug certainty disparaging the idea of a national conscription as practiced by other European countries. But many were less sanguine and expressed a genuine and obvious local concern:

Royal Cornwall Gazette - Thursday 21ˢᵗ August 1890

THE UNFORTIFIED STATE OF FALMOUTH Sir, A just estimate of the coast line of the British Isles seems at the present time to be a question at once important. My attention has of late been drawn to the meager, and, as I apprehend, unsafe condition in which Falmouth would find herself in the event of an attack from some foreign foe….. I would ask of what use is Pendennis or St. Mawes Castle, without a solitary cannon in a fit and efficient state, to cope with such an emergency?….. if any people on the face of this

planet bays cause to breathe the following_ soliloquy — "Sic semper transit gloria mundi,"
it is the people of the quaint little port of Falmouth.

Beside patriotism impetus was again provided by more of the written word as during this time popular stories of naval warfare and invasion fiction proliferated, an example being, in 1888 Hugh Arnold-Foster *In a Conning Tower*, concerning war in a Royal Navy 'Ironclad". This was followed in 1892 by Admiral Philip H. Colomb's *The Great War of 1892* and in 1901 George Griffith *The Raid of Le Venger* that discussed the sinking of the now 'vulnerable' Ironclads.[25] Plus the many works of H.G.Wells including his famous *War of the Worlds*. There were many more such as those by, the now well known author William le Quex who published his new title *The Great War in England 1897* this followed in 1903 by Erskin Childers *The Riddle of the Sands*. In 1906 John Tregellis' *Britain Invaded* competed with le Quex as his *The Invasion of 1910* was serialised in the *Daily Mail* newspaper. All of whom in one way or another told of an unprepared Britain.

One interesting fact concerns the (in)famous *The War of the Worlds* national radio broadcast of 1938 read to the American public by the up and coming actor Orson Wells. Despite many books and even documentaries stating that this caused a 'national panic', this is a fable created by the newspaper industry trying to discredit the 'new' medium of radio and possibly supported by Wells himself as it promoted his name.

For nearly 30 years the Rifle and Volunteer Artillery movement had attempted to run in tandem with the army for home defence and as we have seen, initially meeting some resistance. Now it was recognised that greater integration, financial support and increased professionalism was required and so in 1887 this resulted in the implementation of a brigade structure within the regular army. This arrangement lasted for some 21 years until in 1908 these civilian 'Rifle 'and 'Artillerymen' ceased to exist in their previous forms. Or to put it more succinctly in the words of General Sir Frederick Maurice *'The reorganisation involved many enquiries and much controversy. The greatest of them was the reorganisation of the inchoate mess of Yeomanry, Militia and Volunteers*[26]. For, as we have seen they had evolved in what may be seen in a very British way, similar to its empire, haphazard and never with a properly coordinated master plan.

Changes of that year with The Territorial and Reserve Forces Act made them volunteer part time units[27] within the new Territorial Forces. Later legislation also replaced the militia with the Special Reserve and from 1910 all had been incorporated as the Territorial Force. Like their predecessors these so called 'Terriers' were mostly liable for home service but they would be ordered to fight overseas as front line troops where necessary after the introduction of the second Military Service Act in May 1916 during the Great War[28]. From 1921 their name changed to the Territorial Army and the Special Reserve became known once more as the Militia but after three years the Supplementary Reserve.

Volunteer Yeomanry Cavalry

Volunteer Yeomanry cavalry units operated formally from 1795 to 1921, though smaller, informal troops were common at least through the latter years of the 18th century mainly as internal security units during times of perceived civil unrest[29]. Using two incidents as examples the first that illustrates a disaster and the second where common sense on both sides of the divide prevailed. Firstly the most famous incident and therefore infamous unit were The Manchester and Salford Yeomanry. Their intervention at St. Peters Fields, Manchester on the 16th August 1819 and the resulting deaths and injuries still polarises public opinion even now[30]. The 'Peterloo Massacre' was probably caused by inexperienced, prideful young men atop panicking horses, both lashing out when becoming frightened by the large pressing, noisy crowd. Unfortunately 12 or more of the protesters died and many more were injured.

Secondly, not only were the industrialising cities centres of disturbance about the decline in living standards as the so-called agriculture 'Swing Riots' erupted in the autumn of 1830.

As farming had also began mechanising obviously the main focus of the disturbances were threshing machines that displaced workers. But the protesters also rioted over low wages and the still enforced law of paying tithes to the Church of England. Focusing on financial loss, the county of Kent witnessed the most destructive agitation. Here the workhouses and tithe barns associated with their oppression were destroyed, plus hayrick burning and the maiming of cows. The West Country, although it witnessed unrest, this was never to the level experienced in other southern counties. In north Devon one such incident involved a large group of agricultural workers who assembled and moved from the village of Landkey where they articulated their seemingly well judged grievances to a local magistrate. Their claims were not answered and so from there they travelled to the village of Swimbridge under two miles away, where they were met by senior members of the local authorities and two units of yeomanry.

> **North Devon Journal** - Thursday 16 December 1830
> *.....their cry was for diminution rents and tithes, and though no outrage was committed, their language and conduct was very violent; in the afternoon they arrived at the village Landkey, where they were met John Budd, Esq., magistrate, who enquired into their grievances, and was told them that they could not possibly subsist on the rate of wages paid the masters in those parishes, but they knew that it was riot in "the power of the farmers to advance their wages, unless reduction was made to them in their rents and tithes ; and their object was to endeavour to induce the tithe and land owners to make abatement to their tenants and tithe payers. Strong suspicions are entertained that those persons have instigated and encouraged others, whose duty and interest should have dictated better things. In consequence of this avowal, the necessary precautions were taken by the Lord Lieutenant and authorities of the neighbourhood to deter them from assembling, or counteract their designs; the Swimbridge Troop of Yeomanry Cavalry, commanded Colonel Fortescue and Major Stephens, were early the ground......*

.......and the Fremington Troop of Yeomanry Cavalry was drawn up on the Causeway adjoining Barnstaple Bridge, in readiness, should their services have been required. But we are happy to say the deluded labourers did not again expose themselves legal inflictions; there was just an assemblage of the peasantry, and as far we could ascertain they were for the most part occupied in their usual avocations.

Possibly it was this show of force or that wiser heads prevailed on both sides as the agitators dispersed without violence. However, the authorities later showed a heavier hand by arresting and sentencing the man they perceived to have led the demonstration, James Thome who received an 18 month jail sentence.

Completely separately: of a possible literary connection to these events, a man from Combe Martin, another local village, appealed for calm, understanding and restraint from his fellow farmers and employers. His name was John Ridd: see the famous book, *Lorna Doon*.

The yeomanry's history shows that initially they were raised by the government on a similar basis to the volunteer militia, ordered to serve during times of perceived national threat and internal disturbance and only liable for home service. They were an arm of the state before the establishment of a police force and staffed by those who were financially secure. This held true especially for an officer where the costs were particularly high only more so after 1857 when the government as a cost cutting measure, possibly because of the 1852 Militia Act, began to withdraw central funding. It was in this year that the new Colonel of the Regiment, Lord Ward, paid his Worcestershire Yeomanry from his own pocket[31]. He could afford it as aged 25 in 1842 he inherited an income from property of £200,000 per year[32].

In north Devon their own Yeomanry liked to indulge in patriotic displays which grew *'As the years went by the training of the Yeomanry became a major feature in North Devon's social calendar; Barnstaple Cavalry Week was held in almost the same esteem as Barnstaple Fair'*[33].

North Devon Journal - Thursday 09 June 1853

Thirteen years later a report in the local paper indicates that the annual review of the regiment at Torrington, North Devon again seemed less an expression of the martial state but more a social event indicating a probable widening of the troopers social background. It is interesting to note the influence of the new rifle units:

Great as is the attraction of a Review at all times, so many persons were never known on the ground as on this occasion, to witness the gay scene—the delightful weather being also a great inducement to numbers from distance to visit the open and commanding ground at Bellevue. We hear that when this regiment assembles again, it will be in a new character, as they are to be made Royals and Mounted Rifles. This is a flattering but well-merited compliment to a loyal body of men who have been enrolled as the North Devon Yeomanry for a period of fifty years.

The change to mounted rifles did not happen.

Western Times - Friday 7th January 1870
....the North Devon regiment on parade ground occupied more space honestly, shoulder to shoulder, then any other regiment of an equal number —they were broader shouldered, deeper chested men than most of their fellows—their hearts were so large they wanted plenty of space to give play to the vital organ—and nature had provided them with it, and thus they covered the ground.

Class and 'style' were everything so when aspiring Jewish families wanted to confirm their own rising status they supported and joined their local yeomanry. The Rothschild's of banking fame bought Waddesdon Manor in 1874 and patronized the Royal Buckingham Hussars. However, the lower orders like to make fun of their 'betters' so that this unit were soon given the amusing nickname *'The Flying Foreskins'*[34].

Cornwall did not have its own Yeomanry but those with enough financial means could join Devon's second volunteer cavalry the Royal 1st Devon Yeomanry that had its 'D' Squadron at Bodmin with members from Penzance to Launceston[35]. Be that as it may but reports concerning them were published, especially for a Royal review involving all volunteers:

The Cornish Telegraph - Tuesday 20th June 1876
...so many applications have been received by Sir Garnet Wolseley, that it is estimated that nearly fifty thousand men will be present. Several Yeomanry Cavalry regiments and the Hon. Artillery Company will be among the numbers, and regiments are even coming from Edinburgh to share in the Royal Parade. The large numbers of the Metropolitan Volunteers were dressed in scarlet instead of green, in accordance with the wishes the War Office, and they present much more soldierly appearance......

Although I have written about two incidents involving the yeomanry in relationship to its policing role generally the British public were supportive of these volunteers. The events and ceremonies helped build bonds between serving men and patriotic local populations so despite occasional clashes with crowds, overall regiments were intimately linked to their localities[36]. The volunteers in fact represented a sanitised version of those soldiers who, by conquest were expanding 'their' empire. Therefore not only by this association and safe celebration can we advance the idea that in general the public were surrogate imperialists but also for them a reassurance that if literary fiction became horrible fact the volunteers would repel any invasion; they were in fact in the physical presence of security.

As we have seen in the local newspapers the growth in popularity of Victorian militarism gradually overcame even the resistance of the Liberal stronghold in north Devon and likewise held true throughout most of the West Country. Any differences in this rally to patriotism by the Militia, Rifles or Yeomanry between Devon and Cornwall as has been pointed out can be put down basically to money. Although initially the Cornish were enthusiastic they could not match the enlistment shown by the financially more secure Devon until central government began to supply weapons and other funding.

These various invasion threats and destruction to the home islands that the public read about and the volunteers trained to repel never arose during the majority of the period but their attitudes, and training, would be sorely tested in a country many thousands of miles away in southern Africa.

In the next chapter I will examine the testing of the national viewpoint but mainly the responses of Cornwall and Devon to the Boer War. Also discussed will be the reaction of the British Empire and briefly those of several countries in the international community plus highlighting the abilities of the Militia, Rifle Volunteers and the Yeomanry before and after deployment. I will complete that section by gauging this country's reaction after being made aware of Concentration Camps, by one controversial Cornishwomen whose work and legacy should be more widely known, studied and appreciated.

CHAPTER TWO

"Gentlemen Now Abed?"

Although losing a long, ugly war and its thirteen states in British North America that had united against it after their declaration of independence, an industrial revolution placed Britain ahead of its European neighbours. Its financiers and businessmen then began an attempt to create a new empire. They were assisted by an admittedly relatively small army, later gradually supported by conquered indigenous units and transported by its Royal Navy. This, after Napoleonic Wars, was by far the most powerful in the world and the combination of all enabled the British Isles to grab amazingly large areas of land without recourse to calling for support from the home volunteers. However, in South Africa the Second Boer War (1899 – 1902) was to be very different.

The stated case for the British [Cape Colony] to interfere with the Boer republics was firstly a lack of voting rights for the many hundreds of non-Boers [Uitlanders] who had gone to the southern Transvaal Republic to work the diamond and then the newly discovered gold fields. Secondly, as residents they were also required for 'call up' to their local Boer Commando unit when it engaged in fighting native forces.

Although concessions were offered by the now allied Boer republics of the Orange Free State and Transvaal they were not deemed acceptable by the British Government. Therefore to increase pressure, expecting the republics to give in to their demands, the British announced the sending of 10,000 men immediately to the Cape Colony and the mobilising of its 1st Army Corps.

In Peter Trew's book *'The Boer War Generals'* he writes that *'Much to the relief of the British'* Transvaal president Paul Kruger declared war that officially started on 11th October 1899, having suffered a previous 'civilian' raid mounted by his aggressive neighbours. In fact the British totally underestimated the grit, ability, determination and even the preparedness of their enemy now entering the conflict. For example even in the field of military intelligence their 'farmer enemies' had a budget twenty times greater than its own secret service in south Africa[1]. In fact the intelligence branch of the British army had just thirteen officers and received only £20,000 each year for their efforts throughout the whole empire. Although, even with these limited funds the Director of Military Intelligence, Major General Sir John

Ardagh's branch had compiled a 89 page booklet *Military Notes on the Dutch Republic* containing the numbers and military resources of the republics. But although correctly forecasting they would combine militarily these forces were underestimated as an adversary; unfortunately the report stated that the problem of defending the colonies would be one of just checking 'raids' by two or three thousand Boers[2].

That the later Republic of South Africa brought about the disgraceful Apartheid Acts and, contrary to British law refused to give up their slaves, it should not blind us to the fact that the Boer War was robbery carried out by a society drunk on patriotism, jingoism and the feeling that we had the right to do what we liked, to whom we liked, when we liked.

It was also a painful entry for the British into this, considered by many the first modern conflict. It evolved into a desperately 'dirty' war with little or no concern shown by either side to the black ethnic populations[3] or later by the British to white Boer women and children. It also went on for far, far longer than the expected 'over by Christmas' initially predicted. To the acute discomfort of traditionalists it also revealed some serious flaws in the British military establishment[4].

This was a war of new innovations - *"it must be remembered that smokeless powder, Lee-Metford rifles and Maxim guns were new and untried factors at this time in warfare"*[5]. Consequently, the very brave officers who directed and led their men had to learn lessons and until they did so the British infantry's tactics resulted in needles numbers of casualties, including on many occasions, their own. In a disastrous seven days dubbed Black Week, from 10th–17th December 1899, the British Army suffered three devastating defeats by the Boer republics at Stromberg, Magersfontein and Colenso, with a total of 2,600 men killed, wounded and captured[6]. Followed a month later by Spion Kop when a further 2000 men became casualties[7].

The Cornish Telegraph - Wednesday 6th December 1899
Mr. J. B. Cornish proposed The Navy and Army remarked that it was a long time once the English nation had been engaged in such a great war....They were being told the newspapers that the British victories were being purchased at great expense of life officers and men. The present generation might have grown without knowledge of some of our wars, but it none the less misfortune that such statements should be made and repeated, because they were inclined to frighten the fainthearted and make people think the matter was rather more serious than it was. As a matter fact our present victories were being won at very small loss of life.....

No matter what reassurances were given that this could occur came as a shock. It was alarming both to the general public but especially to its forces waging the war in South Africa under the command of the Devon born General, Sir Redvers Buller VC, the British Army's local Commander in Chief.

Frankly for a time his army and Royal Navy personnel, serving on land, were in dire straits. In time they would need the assistance of extra units of infantry and cavalry from home plus Imperial troops including men from Canada, New Zealand and Australia. There were also many in the medical corps who were Natal Indians, a 1,000 of whom offered their services as stretcher bearers. This included the hospital unit of that later leading light of the Indian National Congress, Mahatma Gandhi[8].

Buller had requested reinforcements after 'Black Week' but he had also asked the government for men from the part time volunteer companies of regular infantry regiments and the Yeomanry. The latter he wanted to act as detachments of mounted infantry, as there were a lack of such troops in this war of movement in the relatively flat and open 'veldt' terrain[9].

These series of defeats had subsequently produced near patriotic hysteria amongst the general British public which transmitted itself to the units Buller had requested, especially the Yeomanry. Consequently when the government called for able-bodied men willing to abandon hearth, homes and families and risk their lives to serve in South Africa[10], many applied. However, the speed of organising such units and the private rising of others by enthusiastic, powerful civilians, who drove a 'horse and carriage' through regulations, caused confusion. Understandably this also created anger and, on occasions, serious disputes between the regular army and some part time volunteer leaders.

There was also an urgent requirement for a change in the law; and also in attitude to those less well off in this rich empire as many men who applied to enlist were turned away as not being considered physically able to be a soldier. In his pamphlet *Efficiency and Reform* journalist Arnold White of the Manchester Weekly Sun gave the actual and shocking figure of 8000 men rejected from 11000 who applied to serve[11]. Figures that go to support the supposition that it was the regularly paid artisan and the middle classes that formed the bulk of the volunteers for South Africa.

Although, as we have seen, none were previously liable for service outside the United Kingdom after the passing of a Royal Prerogative in December 1899 an 'Imperial Yeomanry' was created on the 24th of that month[12]. The initial idea was that the volunteer Yeomanry mounted infantry would be tasked to guard line of communication in South Africa or undertake home service duties enabling the dispatch of more regular cavalry. This was followed by the Volunteers Bill of May 1900 as it was intended that the volunteer infantry would contribute 'Active Service Companies' reinforcing their regular county battalions in South Africa. Even though this bill still could not force any volunteer to serve abroad, as we have seen, many in the country began to sign up immediately. Elements of the Militia and the Riflemen were also used; many for service in South Africa but also for home service to release full time regular soldiers who could then be sent overseas. They were also to process and train the many thousands who volunteered to serve in the army.

One response from the British government was to get rid of Buller whose setback at the battle of Colenso on the 15th of December 1899 sealed his fate. He was replaced by one of the famous British soldier's of the time, this 'Hit Man of the Empire', Field Marshall Lord Roberts. He had more than one reason to question the tactics used in the battle as his only son Lieutenant Frederick Roberts was killed. Roberts brought with him as his Chief of Staff that other famous Briton whose country once again needed him, General Lord Henry Horatio Kitchener of Khartoum.

However, these decisions, on occasion, were met with varying responses. In many areas including Devon and Cornwall, not everyone was judging the events with glassy eyed optimism. Many approached the conflict with hard headed realism. One such comment below came from the commanding officer of the *3rd Volunteers, The Welsh Regiment* who now sounded a cautious and common sense approach:

South Wales Echo - Tuesday 19th December 1899

In the course of an interview which one of our reporters had with Lieutenant-Colonel Gaskell on Monday, the commanding officer of the Cardiff Detachment of the 3rd V.B. Welsh Regiment stated that it was true that several of his comrades had volunteered..... to go to South Africa was no light thing, and many men might be inclined to let their feelings of patriotism overrule their common sense.

Unfortunately, the ideal of 'fighting the good fight' and 'jingo' patriotism saw the re-emergence of issuing white feathers to those deemed not to have the 'right manliness and courage'. How many were persuaded to go by such tactics?

Exeter Flying Post - Saturday 23rd December 1899
THE PREPARATIONS. VOLUNTEER OFFERS.

Four members of the Teignmouth Rifle Volunteers have given in their names as willing to serve in South Africa. The whole of the 22nd Devon Volunteer Artillery has offered its services for garrison duty in the event of the Royal Garrison Artillery (regulars) being required for service abroad.

In Cornwall, as everything is preordained the planning must be first class as God was with us:

The Cornish Telegraph - Wednesday 27 December 1899
THE DINNER. VOLUNTEERS AND THE WAR.

.....Rev. E. B. Keeling (Superintendent Wesleyan Minister, Camborne) replying, referred to the war in South Africa, and said he thought we were doing a very righteous thing in South Africa—(applause)—and believed if the matter was not faced the work of Christianity in that land would put back one knew how many years. (Hear, hear.) He looked upon the operations now being carried out there as a lot of police work to keep our Empire straight, and put down disorder—(applause)—and he had no hesitation whatever in praying most earnestly for the Divine blessing upon the efforts of our troops in that direction, and joined the sorrow and regret that so many lives had sacrificed before the great work was accomplished. (Hear. hear)......

The Reverend Keeling was not alone in his assurances that God supported the Imperial cause, in the capital The Right Reverend Mandell Creighton, Bishop of London told one contingent of the City Imperial Volunteers [CIV] that *"We thank God that in such an hour as this England is at one"*. At Richmond in North Yorkshire Archdeacon, The Venerable William

Danks preached to the Green Howards Regiment Volunteer Service Company that *"This is a righteous war..You are fighting for the equal rights of men in South Africa"*[13]

In spite of these 'heavenly' reassurances, in Cornwall there were however obvious doubts concerning the campaign so far:

Royal Cornwall Gazette - Wednesday 27th December 1899
...... I cannot but think that up to the present our generals, brave as they are— Baden-Powell and one or two others excepted — have been no match for Boer cunning, and the lives of hundreds of brave men have been needlessly and uselessly thrown away. By this time it is fervently hoped that our commanders have learnt a lesson from the enemy, and will do their best to circumvent the Boers In their own game and not go sending our gallant soldiers, until we have no more to send, to attack an impregnable position only to be shot down by an unseen foe like rabbits in a warren.

Maybe because of such articles initial enthusiasm was not seemingly too evident in Penzance even when facing the possibly coercive tactics of one Commanding Officer. Maybe it was a coincidence but a man with the same name who had written the letter concerning minimum casualties to the Cornish Telegraph of 6th December 1899 above.

Cornishman - Thursday 28th December 1899
To receive replies from those who wish to volunteer for active service in South Africa or for garrison duty in England, the commanding officer (Major Cornish) called the officers and men of A. Co. lst V.B.D.C.L.I, on parade at head-quarters in the Penzance Corn Exchange on Friday evening. The men were arranged in sections and individually questioned in the armoury, with the following result : for active service, one officer and three men; for garrison duty, two officers, one staff-officer, four non-commissioned officers, 33 men and 19 buglers. The remainder decided to abide by the conditions under which they joined, viz : mobilise when ordered to do so. The general feeling seemed to be that the War-office should order the whole volunteer force to mobilise.

Again from South Wales there was a note of caution sounded that too much criticism of those not wishing to undertake active service might damage the whole volunteer movement. It also shows disdain concerning possible coercion:

South Wales Daily News - Saturday 30th December 1899
VOLUNTEERS WHO DO NOT VOLUNTEER.

It is needful to protest, very earnestly and strongly, against some of the references made to Volunteers who do not see their way to offer themselves for active service at the present time for, unless the spirit of disagreeable criticisms be promptly checked, very grave injury may be done to the movement which it is so desirable to develop. Probably, only a few Volunteers have been insulted with the silly Christmas card which conferred the Order of the White Feather upon men who have chosen to stay at home rather than go to South Africa.

In Devon sections of volunteers came forward:

Exeter Flying Post - Saturday 30th December 1899
PREPARATIONS FOR THE VOLUNTEER MOVEMENT.

Lieutenant F K Wiedeatt and about thirty of C (Totes) Company have offered themselves for active service. Fifteen men of the South Molton Squadron, I Royal North Devon Hussars out of a total of sixty one, have volunteered for active service in South Africa. It is said that Captain de Las Casas, of the same squadron, will proceed to the front. The Cyclist Section of the Haytor Rifles (5th V.B.D.R) have volunteered for garrison duty, and if necessary for active service. Over a dozen names have been handed in of Torquay Rifles for inclusion with the Volunteers going out to join the Devons in Natal.

Western Morning News - Monday 1st January 1900
WAR AND THE WEST.

DEVON YEOMANRY VOLUNTEERS. About 40 men of the Ist Devon Yeomanry Cavalry, at the Higher Barracks, Exeter, on Monday all volunteered for the front.

The Cornish Telegraph - Wednesday 3rd January 1900
A company 1st Voluntary Brigade Duke of Cornwall's Light infantry(VBDC)

PENZANCE

Number who have volunteered for active service I Officer. 1 Sergeant. 3 Privates : total 5 Number who have volunteered for garrison duty home 2 Officers. I Staff Sergeant. I Sergeants 3 Corporals, 2 buglers, 58 Privates total 67.

HELSTON

*/Captain Pengilly has already volunteered for barrack duty, sixteen men volunteered for the front; the four sergeants offered their service for barrack duty, as did also twenty-eight others of the rank and file.. There were only seven men who from probably very sufficient reasons could not see their way clear to offer themselve**s**.*

PENRYN

Five of the Rifle Volunteers have offered themselves for service in South Africa

Was there the beginning of a certain discomfort at a perceived lack of enthusiasm?

Cornishman - Thursday 4th January 1900
The cream of our volunteer and yeomanry forces will soon be in South Africa, and should a nation turn our attention to the replenishing of the thinned ranks. There are plenty of men who have both the time and the physique for Volunteer work who have never bandied a rifle, and it is be hoped that they will soon fill up the vacant places.

However, evidently elsewhere in the much larger conurbations of the country many men were keen to go:

Newcastle Courant - Saturday 6th January 1900
1st NORTHUMBERLAND VOLUNTEER ARTILLERY. At a meeting of officers of the 1st

Northumberland Volunteer Artillery held at Elswick on Wednesday it was stated that the full complement for the Elswick Battery for service in South Africa had been obtained. There is yet much detail to be arranged, and it will be some time before the battery will be able to leave for the front.

NORTHUMBERLAND FUSILIERS. The following notice has been posted up at the headquarters, St. George's Hall, Newcastle: - "3rd Battalion Northumberland Fusiliers." As a large number of men of this battalion will be sent out to reinforce the regular battalions in South Africa, more men will be required to be summoned.

THE NORTHUMBERLAND CONTINGENT OF THE IMPERIAL YEOMANRY. The following additional subscriptions have been received towards the fund started by Mr. Henry Scott of Hipsburn for the purpose of equipping a force of mounted volunteers in the County of Northumberland for service in South Africa......

Aberdeen Press and Journal - Monday 8th January 1900

*THE ABERDEEN VOLUNTEERS FOR THE FRONT.
TO BE ASSOCIATED WITH THE LONDON SCOTTISH.*

Information has been received in Aberdeen that the War Office authorities have decided to affiliate with the London Scottish the men of the volunteer battalion Gordon Highlanders who have offered themselves for active service in South Africa. It is understood that as soon as the Aberdeen contingent is duly sworn in and equipped they will be dispatched in time to embark along with their comrades

Pall Mall Gazette - Wednesday 10th January 1900
THE VOLUNTEERING OF THE VOLUNTEERS.

The total number of Liverpool Volunteers who have actually given in their names in response to the call to arms is 16 officers and 650 men, all of whom will have to undergo medical examination at Warrington. The preliminary examination in Liverpool has so far been satisfactory. The 5th Irish, who have to furnish a complete company, have sent up 3 officers and over 200 men.

Belfast News-Letter - Thursday 11th January 1900

The entire muster roll, about 800, in command of Lieutenant-Colonel Dick, have volunteered for service in South Africa. The Duke of Connaught, who was accompanied by Major-Generall Gossett, C.B., commanding the Dublin District, received a general salute on arriving at the parade ground. After had made a minute inspection of the ranks, the men were formed up in close order, and the Duke, addressing them, complimented the battalion on the patriotism and good spirit they had shown in volunteering for South Africa.

Northern Echo - Friday 12th January 1900
DEPARTURE 0F THE DURHAM MILITIA.

…..Aldershot correspondent first Militia battalion to leave for South Africa was the 3rd Durham L.I., who were also the first to volunteer for service……

Lord Addington has notified 60 non-commissioned officers and men of the lst Bucks Rifle Volunteers of their selection to form a half-company of the Volunteers 'Company, which is to proceed to South Africa, to join the lst Battalion of the Oxfordshire Light Infantry. …... they are to hold themselves in readiness to proceed to Cowley Barracks, Oxford…..

Shropshire, has now selected a full company of 115 officers and men from the Loyal Battalions of the Rifle Volunteers for duty in South Africa…..

London Evening Standard - Monday 22 January 1900
THE CITY VOLUNTEERS.

The Infantry Contingent of the City of London Imperial Volunteers left on Saturday morning for South Africa. They numbered about 800...amidst an outburst of enthusiasm on the part of the spectators, who not only lined the pavements on each side of the road, but almost filled the windows of the houses along the way.

…….along the narrow part of the Wandsworth Road, the pressure was considerable. A line of flags crossed the road at the end of Nine Elms Lane, and at nearly every house

hereabout there was also a flag or two, and in some cases a good deal of crimson cloth with inscriptions…..

The Volunteer Rifle Corps in the county could be seen by some as indicating at best a form of manly enterprise and at worst 'virtue signalling', especially for those whose incomes prevented them from going to South Africa:

West Briton and Cornwall Advertiser - Thursday 5th April 1900
Capt. Parkin, who was received with loud applause on rising to reply, said personally he would have liked to have gone out with the others—(applause)—but, as Sgt. Kneebone had said, they were not all men of leisure. (Hear, hear.) He was extremely fond of volunteering, which was his hobby—(hear, hear) —but, of course, he felt, and Lieut. Dobell felt, too, that they were both dependent upon their professions for their living, and unless they could live, they could not volunteer. What time they had to spare, however, they were pleased to give to volunteering. (Applause.)

As seen above in some areas of the country there was a near hysterical patriotic rush to volunteer for active service as can be seen by the above newspaper reports, but also the vicious attitude during December 1899 of sending white feather Christmas cards to those who 'should' be volunteering. Only a few caution those willing to offer their services pointing out that enthusiasm might overrule common sense. To sum up, reading the articles from Devon and Cornwall there seems to be some differences in enthusiasm between the counties. This can be explained I believe by the relevant affluence of the former. An affluence shown previously by the numbers enlisting in the volunteer rifle units, those who had a greater stake in society. Neither of course could ever supply the numbers as any given city. But patriotism is a heady wine and many young men seemed to want to show they were made of the Victorian version of the 'right stuff':

Royal Cornwall Gazette - Thursday 12th April 1900
Helston

Since the volunteers have left for the Cape 52 fine young fellows have enrolled themselves among the defenders of their country, and our rifle corps now number 123 members. Never since the formation of the company 40 years ago has there been anything like such a large number in the ranks as at present. England need not fear a foreign - invasion so long as her young men come for- ward so willingly and determinedly to be drilled so as to be prepared in case of need to defend our shores against the attack of an enemy.

Cornubian and Redruth Times - Friday 13th April 1900
It has been suggested that publish from time to time a list of names of Cornishmen who are serving their Country in the South African War. To this end we welcome information from

any quarter. Undoubtedly, hundreds of Cornishmen have volunteered their services to fight the Boers, and hundreds of them must now be engaged in the struggle.

Although the article then goes on to name 54 volunteers, all from the county but, reading the units with which they served, there was a wide variety as some had enlisted in South African units such as the exotic sounding Kaffrarian Rifles and a further nine 'regular' soldiers with various units including the Duke of Cornwall's Light Infantry. I can only see four as belonging to actual Cornish residents and although the above figures are way below the actual number engaged I suspect the last sentence was possibly written more in patriotic hope or encouragement than reality.

Some of the Yeomanry volunteers from Cornwall now serving with their parent unit The 1st Devon Yeomanry [later the 27th Company] exhibited a style of discipline that would not be tolerated in the Regular army and could bode ill for the forthcoming campaign. This possibly indicated the attitude expressed above, it was their 'hobby'. That this was not commented on in the article indicates a complete lack of knowledge not only of the men involved and Captain William Bolitho, but also the writer and probably the readers of the paper:

Cornishman - Thursday 26th April 1900
Devon Yeomanry at the Front

One comrade, thoroughly Cornish by name, had a paper sent to him and was reading about their send-off from Exeter, in the stables, with a crowd of troopers round him. Capt. Bolitho strolled that way and stood up, but no one happened see him. As, who was reading aloud, came to the names of the officers present at the station, he remarked "Oh they are no cop; not worth reading about," and all agreed. Just then Capt. Bolitho said "Now then, you fellows let the officers alone….he and they all laughed.

This hardly sounds like the drilled professionalism they aspired to. One thing that did irk the yeomen, in their new role those below NCO rank were now referred to as 'Privates' and not the more 'posh' Trooper they had coveted.

Looking at the new Imperial Yeomanry in greater detail the force was initially recruited on a county by county basis from members of the existing Yeomanry regiments, to provide approximately 115 men each. In addition a large number of volunteers were recruited from the middle and upper classes. In total there were three contingents raised, the first of approximately 11,000 men arrived in South Africa between February and April 1900 but unfortunately despite previous stipulations not all were found to be proficient in neither horsemanship nor horesmastership. The second, 'new yeomanry' numbering approximately 16,500 that had been recruited early in 1901 and mainly from the working class were very poorly trained as were the third and last comprising about 7,000 recruited in December 1901. A later report stated that up to 75 percent of the middle group had not ridden a horse and the remainder had only ridden a little. Also, not only were they were reported as being generally ignorant of the care and management of horses, what was worse, many were unwilling to learn. It was added that even the elementary training of 3,000 volunteers at the depot of Harrismith, between Johannesburg and Durban, and the training ground at Maitland was so bad that nearly all the officers and 20 percent of the men were sent home[14].

Their ability to learn however convinced many in the regular army that most of these men after a time could be relied on, even Lord Roberts, the Commander-in-Chief who had initially distrusted the volunteers became Honorary Colonel of the City Imperial Volunteers [CIV][15]. General Ian Hamilton under whom the CIV served for much of its time stated that *"They ripened very quickly. They improved before my eyes. They were not normally the type of people who served Britain in a military capacity with most being much better educated. Many came from the professional classes, ran their own businesses or farmed occupations that required a great deal more intelligence than the average 'ranker' or 'trooper'".*

However, some did not have time to 'ripen' which led to a very embarrassing tragedy suffered by the 13th Battalion of the Imperial Yeomanry at Lindley on the 31st May 1900. These men commanded by Lieutenant Colonel Basil Spragge, comprised the 'cream' of the Anglo-Irish establishment. They had been dubbed by the press and public as the 'Millionaires Own' and, as they were well connected only spent one week training at Maitland with many gaining a place on Roberts's staff.

A later enquiry found that this was a preventable fiasco as they could have retreated. Poor judgement resulted in the battalion being surrounded in the town and although most men showed great bravery. For example, Captain the Lord Longford, blood streaming from wounds in his neck, face and wrist ordering his men to fight to the end. Later a gentleman-trooper remarked, *'and not a man refused'*; but the unorthorised rising of a white flag from a different company brought surrender. Spragge's command suffered 19 dead plus four officers and 28 men wounded and another 367 men captured unwounded. In Britain news of the disaster was received with incredulity as four of the prisoners were members of the House of Lords. This thus marked the end of the Imperial Yeomanry's and the country's certainty or assumed superiority[16].

Cornubian and Redruth Times - Friday 27th April 1900
A draft of twenty officers and men being asked for by the War Office from the Cornish Rifle Volunteers to join the Company now the front South Africa.

This was in response to the number of infantry killed and wounded. By June 1900 this list had risen again when it was reported that unfortunately four Volunteers were reported killed from 135 and 20 wounded. Of the other injured Cornishmen three were Yeomanry and a further 27 who were living in the colony and had joined the British South African forces. Also mentioned were six from the St John's Ambulance and the Scillonian, H.L Smith-Dorian of [the later] 1914 Le Cateau fame. Obviously the paper had to rely on people writing to inform them; consequently this list cannot be definitive as to the actual numbers who were in South Africa.

By March1900 the capture of the Orange Free State capital of Bloemfontein in March followed by Pretoria, the Transvaal capital in June led many to believe it was time for home.

For the war had become the most the tiresome and boring duty of seemingly endless patrols or the guarding of slow moving military convoys. Those that thought the war would now be over were soon to be disillusioned shown by a growing disinterest. However, some even as early as September 1900 began to see a need for obvious change and to therefore call for army reform:

Cornish & Devon Post - Saturday 15th September 1900
LESSONS OF THE (Boer) *WAR. Mr. Moulton, Q.C., M.P. for the Launceston Division, addressed the first meeting of his constituents in the present political campaign at Port Isaac on Wednesday last in the Temperance Hall…. because there might come time when we are called upon to defend this country against foreign invasion in fact, there is need for army reform all round.*

What reward for the returning men could be expected?

Totnes Weekly Times - Saturday 20th October 1900
WOUNDED POOR REWARD FOR DEVON SOLDIER. … called to the circumstances of wounded soldier, who appears to have received very scant consideration from the War Office, and whose treatment is not calculated to popularise the Army. The soldier in question is Private Charles Webber, of Barnstaple, No. 4866, member of the Ist Battalion Devon Regiment. … Webber had his knee smashed by an explosive bullet, and, as result of the injury, the limb has been amputated well above the knee. Webber made soldiering the business of his life, and, as consequence, he has no trade, and is practically helpless. We are informed that owing some extraordinary circumstances has been left without any pay for just three weeks—a small matter for officials in Pall Mall, but a very considerable hardship for wounded man without any means. But here a man who permanently incapacitated, and the intimation receives that for 12 months be will get Is 6d a day. See Appendix 3. My research shows this probably occurred on the 21st October 1899 during the Battle of Elandslaagte about 15 miles north east of Ladysmith when the 1st Devons suffered four officers and 29 men wounded 'from a storm of magazine fire'[17].

Although the government offered little in compensation, Professor Ian Beckett in his *'The Victorians at War'* shows that there were several existing charities to which an injured serviceman or his family could apply for help. The *Soldiers and Sailors Families Association* that had been in existence for several years, now gave about £1,000,000 to over 2,000 dependants of men who were or had been serving in South Africa. New charities had also been created plus *The Daily Mail*, *The Telegraph* and other national and local newspapers, villages and private individuals all providing financial support for those servicemen affected by the war.

Unfortunately for all concerned the conflict was far from over. The remaining Boer units adopted what would now be called 'asymmetric warfare' whereby a small force continually damages its much larger enemy by 'hit and run' tactics. In the vast areas of rural South Africa for the British it was extremely boring and tiresome, until suddenly and violently brought under fire. But generally, in the words of Lieutenant Colonel Younghusband '*On the whole a weary, dreary nightmare and not worth writing about*'[18].

Although the Commander in Chief of the Imperial forces in South Africa Lord Robert's left his command in December 1900 stating that the war was 'practically over' a more realistic observation came from a William Power. He was a yeoman Lieutenant of the 8th (Derbyshire) Company that told his family in a letter '*I don't believe this war will be over for a very long time that is if they* [the Boers] *want to go on with it*'[19].

He was correct. On the 13th December 1900 the Devon and Cornishmen comprised the 27th (Devon) Company of the Imperial Yeomanry were part of a large force at Nooitgedacht in the Magaliesberg Mountains west of Pretoria. They were brigaded with two other volunteer units the 20th Fife and Forfar Light Horse and another West Country unit the 26th Dorset. The total force amounting to 1515 men, comprising infantry artillery and Imperial Yeomanry [IY] under the command of Major General Ralph Clements. He was a veteran of campaigns in Africa and Burma and consequently should have known better that to choose the site he did to encamp. Unknown to him this was recognised and consequently his force was about to be attacked by around 3,000 Boers from three different Commandos.

It was the non-existent co-ordination of his enemies' attack that saved his command. But poor staff work of his headquarters ensured that after the assault had started the men of the 27th and 20th IY were placed in great danger. Confusion led to both units climbing a thousand feet from the valley up the only track towards the top of the mountain, with their rifles and bandoliers. Their timing could not have been worse for as they reached the summit the Boers swept forward to the edge of the plateau where they commanded the exit. Realising their danger the IY men dashed out to try and find cover but were shot down, with a Captain of the 20th and Captain W.E.J. Bolitho [see above Cornishman -Thursday 26th April 1900] second in command of the Devons, falling wounded. Jumping over their prostrate bodies, other yeoman ran towards a trench but again received a fusillade of rifle fire, resulting in six deaths and seven wounded from the 20th with the 27th Devons losing five killed and ten wounded. Besides this more than twenty men from both companies who could not escape down the track surrendered. Then, from this advantageous position, the Boers rained down rifle fire on the British below. This obviously caused casualties and not just to the men, but also injuring the IY mascot, a monkey who miraculously survived after being hit three times.

Clements, although to blame for this mounting possible debacle, now showed how experienced he was by blocking the mountain's footpath with rifle armed IY and organising a withdrawal[20]. This saved the day for the majority of his force and saw two men from north Devon, Sergeant Bright and Private Cole being awarded the DCM for bravery. For British morale this was a requisite because, if his force had been defeated and captured, there would have been the biggest loss of the whole war. It would also have caused enormous embarrassment, as it occurred just as a confident Roberts had been replaced by Kitchener.

But the men of the 27th must have had little thanks for Clements. Their and Captain Bolitho's experiences, must have been very different from that envisaged when setting out from their West Country homes less than a year earlier. In fact in many units this seems to have promoted a sense of realism as many men accepted positions in the new colonies establishments leaving the army for better paid civilian occupations. The haemorrhaging of men was so bad that a composite unit had to be created by amalgamating the Devon, including its remaining Cornish contingent, Dorset, Somerset and Surry companies[21]. Thankfully Captain Bolitho recovered from his wounds and having received a promotion to temporary Major in the Army from 18th October 1900 he became an Honorary Major on 29th April 1901 and awarded the DSO on the 27th September 1901.

As the public had believed the war won with the capture of the Boer capitals in March and June 1900, about a year later enthusiasm for the conflict in some areas had waned being replaced with increasing apathy and boredom. I include a more full newspaper report as I believe it indicates an obvious general disinterest after the initial enthusiasm for the war. The first parades of the volunteers in the Spring of 1900 brought brass bands, crowds, hearty flag waving and 'drinks all round for the departing heroes', just 12 months later, in a few places their homecoming was rather different:

St. Austell Star - Thursday 30 May 1901

Mr Hodge…..spoke in the highest terms of the Cornwall Regiment and the regrettable death of Col Aldworth and other officers. In answer to the call for volunteers, 93 went from Cornwall, and of them six were invalided home, five remained in South Africa in civil employment, five joined Kitchener's bodyguard, and three were left behind sick……

J. Stephens, in supporting the toast, said he was sorry to see so few of the townspeople of St. Austell who were ready to cheer the men when they left, not present to give them a band-grip on their return. They were full of enthusiasm, zeal, and admiration when these men were going out to fight for their Queen and country, and it struck him that that enthusiasm should not have been allowed to fizzle out but should have been represented by a large attendance to welcome them home…..

But elsewhere: on the 10th of June at Richmond Sergeant Mackenzie of the Green Howards found that *'Our reception was enthusiastic and we were splendidly and hospitably treated by the Mayor and corporation and indeed by the whole of the inhabitants'.* Likewise Norwich equalled the celebratory mood, it's returning company's march through the streets being accompanied by brass bands and cheering crowds lining the city's streets.

And one small town in north Devon, home town to the brave Sgt. Bright and Pvt. Cole provided the more usual West Country welcome:

South Molton Gazette – Saturday June 15th 1901

A right good hearty welcome was accorded the Volunteers who returned home to their native town on Monday evening from the war. The town presented a good and attractive appearance, flags and bunting being displayed in honour of the occasion. It is intended shortly to further laud and honour the loyal and patriotic volunteers, as well as their comrades who were invalided home and members of the Local (sic) Imperial Yeomanry who have returned from the front, at a public dinner, when it is hoped that some tangible recognition of their arduous service will be made to each member. Mr. F. Merson has generously subscribed £5 towards the fund.

South Molton has been singularly fortunate; six volunteers went out from the town and all have returned safe and sound.

See also http://www.southmoltonmuseum.org/page36.html and https://www.devonheritage.org/Places/DevonCounty/SeargeantWilliamColeDCM.htm

Penzance also had a major celebration upon the return of its 'sons':

Cornishman - Thursday 11 July 1901
PESENTATION OF THE BOROUGH FREEDOM TO PENZANCE VOLUNTEERS. AN AUSPICIOUS EVENT. The spacious hall, which forms the principal part of the Penzance public-buildings has, since its erection has seen the scene of many noted gatherings, but on no occasion bas any assembly been of such historic interest as that which met within its granite walk on Tuesday evening, when those brave volunteers who had served their country by aiding its war against the Boer rebellion were rewarded with the highest dignity the town can confer any of its most worthy citizens—the freedom of an ancient and loyal borough. Twas (sic) an event which will long be remembered in Penzance and neighbourhood because of its auspiciousness. Mr. Edward Main, who was received with cheers, said he felt sure no words of his would be needed to recommend to their cordial acceptance the toast which he had the honour to propose—the Army, Navy, and Reserve Forces; and he was also sure no words of his could do adequate justice to the toast. He was sure that One - and - All would hail the arrival of that day and when it came would believe that the many sacrifices which we had been compelled to make had not been made in vain. (Hear, hear.) He was glad indeed to be present that evening, to take some part in that important gathering and to join in the welcome which Penzance were giving to the local volunteers. (Applause) They were proud of their achievements, of the patriotism which they displayed, and the response they made to the call of Duty when asked o depart from our midst. He was much struck by a remark made by his good friend, Major Bolitho, on the occasion of his return home. It was an utterance characteristic the man (Applause.) He said he did claim anything great for himself. He only claimed that at the call of Duty, he—like thousands of others, thank God—responded to the call and did their best. (Applause)

However, as the war dragged on as we have read sections of the public were displaying a marked disinterest. One letter appealed to their 'better angels':

<u>Cornish & Devon Post</u> - Saturday 12<u>th</u> October 1901

Whatever we may think of the justice of the war, the mistakes of our generals, or the want of training on the part of the regimental officers, there is one point on which we must be all agreed. Our soldiers, under the most trying circumstances, have behaved admirably throughout a series of campaigns in a war now entering on its third year. The biggest army that Great Britain has ever sent abroad has exhibited all the qualities of a British army. It has done its duty, and been found ready to die whenever the final sacrifice of its gallant blood has been required. In short, whatever our politics may be, we have every reason to be proud of our soldiers. This is fact that we cannot afford to forget. They are fighting to-day with the same unbroken gallantry they exhibited in the first few months of the war, when they were supported by and conscious of the enthusiasm of shouting crowds and the whole admiring attention of the country. But since 'Tommy' sailed light heartedly to 'wipe something off slate', many things have happened. .... we are already paying in the form of apathy and fatigue The public has grown so accustomed to the war that it takes it as matter of course....... Let us show that, at least, we do not forget, and straggle against the selfish indifferences begotten of weariness of a thankless task.

A thankless task indeed as what followed was a war of attrition undertaken by many of the Boers who refused the call to surrender, the so called 'Bitter Enders'. Consequently, as the war dragged on and became an international embarrassment a few months into his command an exasperated Kitchener implemented a system of 'sweeps' that involved the distasteful task of burning farms and putting, or concentrating, their recalcitrant families in camps. Ultimately this worked but with most of the world's public, who displayed great sympathy for the Boers, condemning such policies as deplorable bringing an increase in ground level anglophobia. However, in respect of their own interests the most governments of the major powers, who were entangled in imperialist adventures of their own, held back from outright condemnation[22]. Prior to the war there had been exceptions with Imperial Germany's Kaiser Wilhelm the Second's famous or infamous telegram to the President of the Transvaal Paul Kruger of the 3rd of January 1896. This congratulated Kruger for the defeat of a ham-fisted attempt by military adventurers led by Leander Star Jameson to overthrow his government by a military coup. As Britain considered the republic within its 'sphere of influence' this was considered by them, in a phrase of the time 'Bloody Cheek' and is rightly considered another speed bump on the road of good relations with Germany.

In the morning of Saturday 31st May 1902 at Vereeniging in the Transvaal Boer delegates from the two republics voted for a treaty created by Kitchener. It passed by 56 votes to 6 with the final surrender agreements being signed at 11pm that evening. All then retired to their hotel rooms, the Boers to commiserate but the British to celebrate especially Kitchener whose £50,000 victory grant awarded by Parliament he asked to be converted into gold shares[23]. Insider dealing one suspects, on a grand scale.

North Devon Journal - Thursday 12 June 1902

THANKS GIVING SUNDAY. BARNSTAPLE. Practically the whole of the Churches and Chapels in Barnstaple peace thanksgiving services were held on Sunday. The memorial service at the Parish Church was attended by the A and B Companies of the 4th V.B.D.R., with the battalion band, the officers present being Capt. Ashton, Lieut. Brown and Capt. and Adjutant Campbell. Included in the very large congregation were also several returned Volunteers and Yeomen from South Africa, including Capt. Eyton (Imperial Yeomanry). The sermon was preached by the Vicar (the Rev. Dr. Newton). If such nations as Germany, England, and Russia, who were armed to the teeth, resolved that war should not happen, the peace of the world to great could lie secured. He enlarged on the blessing of peace with the Boers, and said already there were signs that the Briton and the Boer would fast friends and brothers, and that South Africa would become a most prosperous Colony under our King. In many respects the War had been a blessing in disguise.

Who were the Volunteers?

The war was over, but how many volunteers born in the two counties were involved? It's complicated as some had moved to the county and joined while others had moved from the county and joined their now local voluntary groups. See the Morrab Gardens Penzance Boer memorial for clear examples of these men. However, I have discovered the excellent Anglo-Boer War website https://www.angloboerwar.com/ that lists the 27th Company of the 7th Battalion active as mounted infantry being 'sponsored' by the Royal North Devon Hussars and the Royal 1st Devon Yeomanry. The latter will have contained not only Devonians but also Cornishmen of their 'D' Squadron based at Bodmin, Cornwall.

Apart from this we have the report in the St Austell star of the 30th of May 1901 that states... *in answer to the call for volunteers, 93 went from Cornwall* – this, I think, refers to infantry but I have not been able to determine a definitive number as so many people from the West Country were already living in the colony. We know a number had previously joined their armed forces, such as the Kaffrarian Rifles, recorded above in the Cornubian and Redruth Times of Friday the 13th April 1900. For Devon again my research cannot arrive at a firm answer.

For both it should be remembered that this was the first Imperial war where the colonies of New Zealand, Australia (a colony up to 1901) and the Dominion of Canada were enthusiastic about sending men to fight against the Boers. It is distinctly possible as with the Great War, that a number of these men were immigrants from the West Country.

As to cost, this was the first modern war using weapons that were invented in the late 19th Century who's 'efficiency' caused high casualty rates and dominated the conflicts of the 20th. This was also the last major action involving the British Empire's soldiers in which far more men died from disease than battle. 20,721 died during the war of which 63 percent, 13,139 were from illness and disease, especially 'Enteric Fever', typhoid. A minor confirmation of this can be seen on the above mentioned Penzance Boer War Memorial in Morrab Gardens that lists eight casualties, divided equally between military action and illness. An estimation of Boer casualties puts their fighters' deaths at 7,000[24]. Finally, monuments at Truro Cathedral list the names of 192 Cornishmen but these obviously record both regular soldiers as well as the volunteers. Exeter Cathedral has two very large Salacian marble tablets that lists 300 Devonians who died during the war with the vast majority recorded as serving with the regular soldiers of the Devonshire Regiment[25] including nine from their Voluntary Service Company [VSC] and one from Cheshire VSC.

Concentration Camps

One aspect of the war that I will touch upon and that received increasing inches in local newspapers concerned Concentration Camps, an aspect that does have a very deep but rather unknown Cornish connection. As we have seen above these had been set up by the British to keep Boer women and children off their farms and away from their sons and husbands, the so called 'Bitter Enders' as we have seen who continued the fight even after the surrender of most Boer forces and the capture of both capitals.

The term 'concentration camps' was first used by two radical MPs C.P. Scott and John Ellis taking it from the notorious *reconcentrado* camps set up by the Spanish to deal with Cuban guerrillas during the fight for Cuban independence[26].

It was alleged by campaigners, including the Cornishwoman Emily Hobhouse that women and children were dying at an alarming rate of disease and mistreatment.

Cornishman - Thursday 09 January 1902
......replied to question addressed him on the subject of the concentration-camps, that there was no use in endeavouring to do anything for the children because they had all died in the camps. This statement, which Dr. Kuyper must have known to be untrue, appeared simultaneously in the Times with a record of the educational work carried on in the concentration-camps, by which it was shown that no less than 14,000 children were receiving an education superior to anything they had known under the regime of Mr. Kruger.....

Not all were so sanguine

North Devon Journal - Thursday 09 January 1902
UNIONISM BARNSTAPLE. SPEECHES BY THE HON.W PEEL..... They were compelled to burn farms because they were made arsenals for every roving Boer commando. But this was not policy—it was necessity. (Applause) The women and children who were thus left homeless were placed in camps formed for them, and they were fed even better than our own troops. (Applause) Why, instead of having adopted methods of barbarism, they had, as it turned out, done too much the way of leniency. Instead of there being any justification for the charges of barbarism, they had done more than had been done in any previous war to conduct matters with the utmost leniency and with the utmost humanity. (Cheers) These

concentration camps had been talked a good deal about and they were told that they ware
sacrificing the lives of the women and children, but of course the critics did not say a single
word to the difficulties under which they had laboured, not a single word as to the sanitary
habits of the women and children congregated in those camps. (Applause)

Cornubian and Redruth Times - Friday 17th January 1902
The Mining Division. Meeting at Camborne

…..disastrous failure, gross, wicked incapacity and blunders which were worse than crimes,
but which were crimes, in the conduct the war, the dealing with our own soldiers in the field,
the dealing with our enemies and enemies wives and children in the concentration camps and
elsewhere. (Cheers)

Feelings were running high in this letter from an ex-pat now living in South Africa who
had suffered, he alleged, depredations during the war carried out by the Boers:

Lake's Falmouth Packet and Cornwall Advertiser - Saturday 18th
January 1902
Even now the mother country was nursing the viper. In the concentration camps, where they
were receiving food and clothing from England, the Boer mothers were teaching their children
to vow vengeance. Lord Roberts a good general was, (sic) had made one mistake. Instead of
providing for the Boer families, he should have forced them back on the Boer commandoes for
them to place on neutral ground and to provide for them in the writer (sic).

Emily Hobhouse, Cornish borne and a great 'Rights for Women' and welfare campaigner
began to be noticed:

Western Morning News - Tuesday 21st January 1902
In the British Parliament *"It was gross misrepresentation of the fact to that the majority*
of the women and children had gone into the concentration as a place of refuge, far the greater
number of them having been brought there and kept here as prisoners of war. By the operation
of those camps 10,000 Boer children had lost their lives in the last eight months, and that
was due mainly to overcrowding, insufficient shelter and unsuitable food; and that the state
of things would have gone on but for exposure of Miss Hobhouse". (Irish Nationalist Cheers).

Although her motives are above reproach it was focused on one group of the racial divide.
It should be understood that Emily Hobhouse, although apparently sympathetic to the plight
of the indigenous people in camps equally if not worse than those that held the Boer families,
did little to ameliorate it.

Not only Kitchener's oppressive 'sweep' policies but also Boer Commando raids dispossessed
African families who initially came to the British for protection, hence their concentration in
camps. Although this then provided the army with poorly paid workmen who were away for

up to three months at a time, it was also beneficial to the local white administration. They needed men to work in the now reopened mines, labour that also took the men away from their families for varying lengths of time. Unfortunately the women and children left in the camps and living, as were the Boers in 'bell' tents, because of appalling neglect and poor administration, this caused sickness and despondency then diseases that swept through the camps causing a soaring death rate. In the six months between June and December 1901 well over 8,000 deaths were recorded, but in all probability there were many more that went unremarked. One visiting clergyman mused that, *"unlike the Boer women they have no champion to plead for them"*, adding they were *"bound to go to the wall"*[27].

At this time Emily Hobhouse totally identified with the Boer *'vrouw'* or wife, white women like herself. For example she added one further recommendation in a letter to the *Times* who published it in late June 1901 *'Considering the growing impertinence of the Kaffirs, seeing the white women thus humiliated, every care shall be taken not to put them in places of authority'*. Coming from her this was exceptionally wrong. When commenting on black people in private she was careful, even in her letters to her Boer friends, to avoid such language. What it does reflect, though, is her passionate dedication to the Boer cause, a dedication which blinded her to all other considerations[28]. Such also were the attitudes of her audience, racial intolerance and arrogance seemingly being the mindset from the Castle to the Cottage or Campsite within the British and other European and North American empires.

An estimation of 28,000 non-combatants died in the camps containing Boer civilians, the vast majority being children. The African death toll is harder to calculate as noted above so many deaths went unrecorded or unremarked, however, the latest (1999) figures are that of the 115,000 interned 20,000 died. There were also many who, while assisting the British as scouts or *agterryers,* an Afrikaans word meaning a mounted assistant, were shot out of hand by the Boers[29]. Also, maybe at times it seems by the British. At the end of one lost battle it was simply recorded that two local guides, who the report blamed for leading their soldiers along the wrong track were shot, with no other explanation provided as whom exactly pulled the trigger.

Previously on the 28th July 1894 one man spoke for generations of Africans dispossessed by white settlement. Chief Mmalebogo of the Ganawa branch of the Sotho people lay under siege by the Boers after refusing to give in to their demands. At night in an attempt to bring water to his thirsty followers he was fired upon by a Boer picket after which he shouted to them, his words possibly being translated by a Swazi auxiliary *"You have taken from me my women and children, my cattle and my corn ; my villages you have burned. Now you will not let me even have a drink of water; wait until tomorrow and you shall have me, what do you seek in fighting tonight"*[30]. Ultimately he and his small number of mainly non-combatant followers were starved out, he was arrested and his people distributed as servants among Boer farms.

Unfortunately the iniquities of this so called 'White Man's War' of poor leadership, concentration camps and the shooting of prisoners that were now being exposed seemed to worry only a small minority of the literate classes.

The popularity of the volunteers within the country reached great heights as we have seen during the war, so much so that the militia grew in size and twelve new yeomanry units were formed, some even in counties that had not previously fielded any. Cornwall was not one of them; and Devon retained its two, the Royal North Devon Hussars and the now 1st Devon 'Imperial' Yeomanry, but with the addition of a sizeable number of new Cornish recruits:

Cornish Guardian - Friday 16 May 1902
THE VOLUNTEERS. CORNISH YEOMANRY. The first annual shoot of the D Squadron of the Royal Ist Devon ImperialYeomanry took place at Hayle and Wadebridge last week. This squadron composed of Cornish Yeomanry and its strength of 74 includes young farmers resident in the district from Camelford to Helston. Practically the whale of the squadron competed in the shooting, with 24 of the competitors being trained men and the rest recruits. Major Bolitho. D. S.O., Major Williams, Captain and Adjutant Lethbridge and Squadron Sergt.-Major Chew were in attendance.

However, just two weeks before came a decision affecting those less well off:

Western Times - Friday 02 May 1902
A new War Office regulation is calculated to sound the death knell of rifle practice artisan corps by making ammunition too expensive for the average Volunteer to buy.

Be that as it may but more importantly the crisis of confidence in its regulars' strength, prowess and organisation led to great changes in the structure of the British Army. Unfortunately as we can see however, it did not lead to a change in overall post war government parsimoniousness.

There was however a change in international relations with an ending of British 'Splendid Isolation'. The Prime Minister Lord Salisbury had reached out via benign neutrality to the USA while that country was engaged in its own imperial land grab during the Spanish – American War of 1898[31]. Also, this new policy then led to the 'Entente Cordial' of 1904 with the French. This was followed three years later with their allies the Russians, as the growth of German sea-power from 1898 contributed to the insecurity of the age[32].

CHAPTER THREE

It's The Same Old Tommy And The Same Old Jack?![1]

After the Act of Union in 1707 with Scotland and 1801 with Ireland the now British Army remained a fully volunteer force and emerged victorious along with its allies against the French during what has been termed the 'First World War'. The Seven Years War 1756 – 1763 saw a global conflict including India, mainland Europe and North America. But shortly after as we have seen above it then suffered defeat as British forces lost what was to become the United States to the Americans and its now French allies during the so called 'Revolution of 1776'. Some 49 years later during the Napoleonic Wars however its army had been a part of the winning coalition that ended in 1815. Over several years following its victory, because of its growing reliance on its navy, the government of Great Britain then downsised this relatively small force. It was only able to police its growing empire when supported by conquered indigenous peoples whose men were officered by the British.

In parliament its size in relation to the very large conscript armies of potential enemies on the European continent caused some considerable political friction over the next 100 years as to the question of conscription.

Although, with the French, we had been victorious in the Crimean War 1854 -1856, because of atrocious mismanagement there was recognition that a thorough reorganisation had to be implemented. Consequently reforms were enacted over the next 40 years by three Secretaries of State for War, firstly Edward Cardwell's from1868 to 1874, Hugh Childers in 1881 and the even greater changes brought about by the Haldane Reforms of 1907.

I will examine how the second reorganisation affected the infantry of the period by looking at our local regiments both of which had an illustrious history to match any in the British Army. Firstly the Duke of Cornwall's Light Infantry in some detail and then the Devonshire Regiment. I will look at the different classifications and conditions of service in 1914 between a full time Regular infantryman, a Territorial or men of the Special reserve etc.

The Duke of Cornwall's Light Infantry

Battles recorded on their colours include Gibraltar 1704-5, Detttingen, Rolica, Salamanca, Peninsula, Waterloo, Sevastopol, Tel-el-Kebir to name but a few. In 1881 the line infantry regiments underwent a major change imposed on them by the afore mentioned Secretary of State for War Hugh Childers — the final stage of the earlier Cardwell's Reforms started in the 1870s.

Their aim was to centralise the power of the War Office, abolish purchase of officers' commissions, and to create reserve forces stationed in Britain by establishing short terms of service for enlisted men. Regiments were also combined to provide a two battalion system. Its two battalions consisted of the 46th (South Devonshire) and the 32nd (Cornwall Light Infantry) Regiment. The latter's elite Light Infantry status had been granted after the Indian mutiny during which their stout defence of the Lucknow Residency during two sieges from May to November 1857 earned three Victoria Crosses. Their new name now included the son of Queen Victoria, the Duke of Cornwall, the future Edward the V11, hence The 32nd Duke of Cornwall's Light Infantry Regiment. It also retained its red over white hackle to denote the 46th victory over the American Rebels at Brandywine Creek in September 1777. Logically it was decided that Victoria Barracks, Bodmin, now The Keep and Museum of the DCLI would be the 'new' regiment's base.

The first battalion served in Malta and at home while the second saw service at Gibraltar and fought in Egypt during the 1880s followed home service in England and Ireland then fought in South Africa during the second Boer War (1899 – 1902) at Paardeburg in 1900 and helped in the capture of Bloemfontain. Garrison duties followed at Gibraltar, Bermuda, South Africa and Hong Kong.

The 1st moved to the Indian subcontinent in 1888, where it stayed for 17 years including anti-guerilla operations in Burma, the North West Frontier in the Khyber Pass and Peshawar areas and guarding of Boer prisoners in Ceylon (now Sri Lanka). It then garrisoned Ireland and the South Africa.

The 1st DCLI were part of the British Expeditionary Force. This comprised two Corps, 1st commanded by Lt General Sir Douglas Haig and the 2nd, from the Battle of Mons, commanded by Lt General Sir Horace Smith-Dorian. The battalion was an integral part of 2 Corps which comprised the 3rd and 5th Infantry Divisions. Each Division had 3 Infantry Brigades each comprising four infantry battalions. The battalion being part of 14th Infantry Brigade[2]

The 2nd DCLI were in 1914 stationed in Hong Kong, but were soon to be called back.

Locations served by the battalions of the Duke of Cornwall's Light Infantry during WW1.

Number Battalion	Western Front	Italy	Salonika	Middle East	India	Home
1st Battalion	Yes	Yes				
2nd			Yes			
3rd						Yes[3]
1/4 Territorial				Yes	Yes	
1/5 (T)	Yes[1]					
2/4 (T)					Yes	
2/5 (T)						Yes
3/4 (T)						Yes
6th Service	Yes					
7th (S)	Yes					
8th (S)			Yes			
9th (S)						Yes
10th (S)	Yes[2]					
11th (S)						
12th (S)						
13th (S)	Disbanded. Absorbed into the Somerset L.I.					

1. April 1916 : moved to Tidworth and converted into a Pioneer Battalion, under orders of 61st (2nd South Midland) Division.

2. Raised at Truro and trained as a Pioneer Battalion. Landed at Le Havre 22nd May 1916 and attached as Pioneers to 2nd Division. 16 July – 7 November 1917: temporarily attached as Pioneers to 66th (2nd East Lancashire) Division. 8th November returned to the 2nd.

3. The Royal Cornwall Rangers Militia whose Boer War nomenclature remained throughout WW1. The battalion never left the UK being stationed on the south coast for the duration of the conflict. It was purely an administrative and training battalion feeding the healthy to active units but also in receipt of the sick or wounded. The battalion's record in 'Soldiers Died in the Great War' p 24 has only 'Home' as the place of death.

The Devonshire Regiment

Initially raised in June 1667 changes in the political situation of the period meant that it only became a permanent part of the army in1685 to defend Bristol against the Duke of Monmouth's rebellion. Swearing allegiance to William and Mary its first action came in Ireland at the Battle of the Boyne in July 1690 against the Irish Army of the deposed James II. It then saw service under the Duke of Marlborough in both Holland and the Iberian Peninsula during the War of Spanish Succession 1701 -1714. Returning to Britain it helped put down the Jacobite rising of 1715, not moving abroad until deployment to Flanders in summer 1742 for service in the War of Austrian Succession 1740 – 1748. Twelve years later once again the regiment embarked for the continent in the spring of 1760 for service in the Seven Years War, at the end of which it garrisoned the island of Menorca.

|Throughout this time it had served under the name of its various Colonels until 1751 when the numerical system of regimental designation was adopted, now becoming the 11th Regiment of Foot. In 1782 it was given the additional county title of 11th (North Devonshire) Regiment.

The 11th spent the early years of the French Revolutionary or Napoleonic Wars serving as detachments in the Mediterranean with the Royal Navy, but in 1809 it deployed to fight in the Peninsular War until 1814. Then, like many of its contemporaries, the 1st Battalion spent most of the 19th century on garrison duty throughout the Empire.

Although the regiment was not fundamentally affected by the Cardwell Reforms of the 1870s, except a permanent depot at Topsham Barracks in Exeter from 1873, or by the Childers reforms of 1881 – as it already possessed two battalions so there was no need for it to amalgamate with another regiment. However, after the reforms it became the Devonshire Regiment from 1 July 1881.

The 1st Devons were stationed in Jersey at the wars outbreak and joined the British Expeditionary Force' [BEF] 8th Brigade 3rd Division 14th September 1914. They were one of the strongest battalions within the division as they had been spared the harrowing retreat from Mons but now in France faced the Battle of the Aisne. On the 30th a move from that area and a transfer to 14th Brigade 5th Division saw them alongside the 1st DCLI. As with all of their comrades within the much depleted BEF, both faced the fighting during this so called 'Race to the Sea', especially the infamous La Bassee area, until finally for 1914, the terrible first Battle of Ypres in Belgium.

The 2nd Devons were in Cairo and guarding the vital Suez Canal until relieved upon which they were shipped to the UK and placed in the newly formed 8th Division 23rd Brigade. Landing in France on the 16th of November 1914 and then proceeded to the Ypres Salient.

The history of the Devonshire Regiment 1914 – 1918 draws the reader's attention to the fact that the wet, muddy and freezing cold conditions in the area in general and the trenches in particular were so bad that 'Coming from warm climates….while their casualties in action were under 20, sickness accounted for over 70.

Locations served by the battalions of the Devonshire Regiment during WW1.

Number Battalion	Western Front	Italy	Salonika	Middle East	India	Home
1st Battalion	Yes	Yes				
2nd	Yes					
3rd						Yes
1/4 Territorial				Yes	Yes	
1/5 (T)	Yes			Yes	Yes	
1/6 (T)				Yes	Yes	
1/7 (T) Cyclist						Yes
2/4 (T)				Yes	Yes	Yes
2/5 (T)	Disbanded in Egypt 1916			Yes		
2/6 (T)				Yes	Yes	
2/7 (T) Cyclist						Yes
4th Reserve						Yes*
5th Reserve	Absorbed by the 4th September 1916					
6th Reserve	Absorbed by the 4th September 1916					
6th Service	Yes					
3/7th (T)	Disbanded in Britain March 1916					Yes
8th (S)	Yes	Yes				
9th (S)	Yes	Yes				
10th (S)	Yes		Yes			
11th (Reserve)	Yes		Yes			
12th (Labour)	Yes					
13th (Works)						Yes
14th (Labour)	Yes		Yes			
15th	Formed from 86th Provisional Battalion January 1917					Yes
16th	Formed January 1917 from the Royal 1st and Royal North Devon Yeomanry. Served in Egypt, Sinai and the Western Front					
1st Garrison				Yes		
2nd Garrison						Yes
51st Graduated	Formed from 206 Graduated battalion					Yes
52nd Graduated	Formed from 210 Graduated battalion					Yes
53rd Young Soldier	Formed from 35th Young Soldier battalion					Yes

*Ireland

The British Infantry

In 1908 the Army underwent further reforms in light of its experience during the Boer War and were instigated in the main by the Secretary of state for War Richard Burton Haldane between 1906 and 1912 against some resistance. As we have seen the reserve forces were reorganised by the Territorial and Reserve Forces Act [passed 1907] and the Militia was renamed the "Special Reserve", with the duty of providing trained recruits in time of war.

The volunteer battalions became part of the new Territorial Force, which was organised into 14 infantry divisions which were called upon to serve abroad. As with other regiments[3] on the 1 April 1908 the D.C.L.I. three reserve battalions were accordingly redesignated as the 3rd (Special Reserve) Battalion at the regimental depot, the 4th (Territorial Force) Battalion at New Bridge Street in Truro and the 5th (TF) Battalion at Honey Street in Bodmin.

What were the new contractual conditions or conditions of service a new infantry recruit signed up for? A man could join the army as a professional soldier of the *regular army* and serve for seven years with 'the colours' and five in the reserve[4], artillery and cavalry units were different. For example in the artillery it was for 6 years plus 6. He could become a part-time member of the *Territorial Force*[5] or as a soldier of the *Special Reserve*[6] and finally, there was the opportunity to join the *National Reserve*[7].

Regular A man wishing to join the army could do so providing he passed certain physical tests. He had to be taller than 5 feet 3 inches, aged between 19 and 38 who would enlist at the Regimental Depot or at one of its normal recruiting offices. The man did have a choice over the regiment he was assigned to. In 1914 the total number of regular soldiers serving in all parts of the British Army amounted to 247,000 men plus the ex Regular Reserves returning to the colours which stood at 145,350 strong.

The Territorial Force: The TF came into existence in April 1908 as a result of the reorganisation of the former militia and other volunteer units. Haldane had received great resistance to its establishment from both the right and left so in order to get it through Parliament its role was limited to home defence and not as immediate reinforcements for the regular army[8]. Although they were enlisted on the basis that in the event of war they could be called upon for full-time service −'embodied'- unless they signed for Imperial Service which entitled them to wear a special badge on their uniform. This changed as from May 1915 with the second Military Service Act cancelling the right for home defence service only status.

Most county regiments of the infantry formed two Territorial battalions. These units were recruited locally and became more recognised and supported by the local community than the regulars. Recruits had a choice of regiment, but naturally the local nature of the TF meant that in general the man joined his home unit. Men trained at weekends or in the evenings and went away to a summer camp. The physical criteria for joining the Terriers were the same as for the Regular army but the lower age limit was 17 years. In May of 1915 this was brought into line with the Regular forces.

Unfortunately the TF was not a popular peace time commitment despite the best efforts of King Gorge V and overall started the war 36,000 men below establishment with only five complete units volunteering to serve abroad[9].

I suspect this lack of popularity compared to the enthusiasm shown by the Victorians Rifle Volunteer Movement 1859-1908 (see above Volunteer Infantry and Artillery) came about because the new battalions lost that immediate local, even intimate status *for the lower middle and artisan classes*[10]. For example after central government investment Cornwall had 20 Rifle (Infantry) companies, two alone in Truro and one each in Falmouth and Penryn, two small towns that still abut one another. There were also 10 Artillery units, including one each for the community of St Just and the tiny village of St Buryan[11].

Although Ian Becket states that it *'proved itself a useful auxiliary to the regular Army in the South African War'*[12] seemingly their direct decedents in the west country were not very popular with Kitchener. He immediately moved the TA Wessex Brigade to India, swopping them for Regular units. Obviously these men had either previously agreed to serve overseas but many did not for various reasons; one concerned training. Because of the *'absurdly insufficient training done by the Territorial Force under peace conditions'* the Suffolk Yeomanry for example faced problems convincing their men to agree. Another example is the 1/4th Northamptons that, when asked only 200 of the potential 950 men volunteered. It took much persuasion by their company commanders to bring this up to 800[13].

In time and after extensive training one of the two India bound Cornwall 'Terriers' served operationally in the near east. One other, out of a total of five [see below] converted to a Pioneer unit and served with some distinction on the Western Front.

Special Reserves: The Special Reserve provided a form of part-time military service. It was introduced in 1908 as a means of building up a pool of trained reservists in addition to those of the regular Army Reserve. These soldiers enlisted for 6 years and had to accept the possibility of being called up in the event of a general mobilisation and to undergo all the same conditions as men of the Army Reserve. This meant that it differed from the Territorial Force (below) in that the men could be sent overseas. Their period as a Special Reservist started with six months full-time preliminary training [paid the same as a regular] and they had 3-4 weeks training per year thereafter. A man could extend his SR service by up to four years, but could not serve beyond the age of 40. A former regular soldier whose period of Army Reserve obligation had been completed could also re-enlist as a Special Reservist and serve up to the age of 42. In 1914 the Special Reserves provided just over 64,000[14] men.

The National Reserve: The National Reserve was a register maintained by Territorial Force County Associations. Registration was voluntary but complex rules of eligibility applied. Its strength as at 1 October 1913 was 215,000 of all ranks. They were not required to undertake any definite liability but were invited to sign an honourable obligation to present themselves for service when required. They would be used to reinforce existing units of the regular army or of the Territorial Force once it had mobilised. It would also be used to strengthen garrisons, guard vulnerable points, provide specialists or tradesmen in technical branches, or be used in hospital, veterinary, remount, clerical or recruiting duties.

Mention also must be made of the large number of voluntary organisations that sprang up for the defence of the home islands, The Volunteer Training Corps. Rather like the 'Dads Army' of the Second World War it attracted, by the time of the Armistice an estimated 234,800 officers and men[15]. They had names that reflected their role such as the Ilfracombe Volunteer Training Corps or the Camborne V.T.C. and the Carrickfergus Athletes Volunteer Force[16]. Only one unit was engaged in combat, this being on the 24th April 1916 during the Easter Rising. In Haddington Road, Dublin the Dublin Veterans' V.T.C. came under fire from men of the Irish Volunteers who killed five men including their commander Frank Browning and wounded another 46[17].

Young Officer's Initial training

Haldane had also brought about change concerning the lower, initial 2nd Lieutenant ranks, within the army. It is so reflective of the times that the Officers' Training Corps had the aim of creating a pool of reserve officers restricted to elite Public Schools and universities. These did in fact fulfil the hope that its advocate and creator had envisaged for it, despite the protests of Ramsay MacDonald, who saw it as a class divider[18]. In total the various OTC's provided 20,500 commissions during the first seven months of the war[19]. In fact during his first leave, Haig arriving in London on the 22nd November 1914[20], advised that the country should send out young Oxford and Cambridge men as officers as *'they understood the crisis facing the British Empire'*[21].

As we have seen above the regiment like most others in the small but well trained British Army comprised three battalions, basically the 1st and 2nd Battalions for operations and the 3rd recruiting men for the other two. In August 1914 the 1st was in Ireland and the 2nd Hong Kong with the 3rd at the base depot in Bodmin. Here they had been responsible for the absorption of the Reserves called back to serve as dictated by their contract upon leaving the army.

If we take the DCLI during the Great War the regiment grew as did other Army units, exponentially, supplying a total of 16 numbered battalions. Battalions 1 and 2 were 'regular – full time', volunteer units, the 3rd recruiting and retraining.

Then came five units of the Territorial Force who were 'part time' volunteers undergoing basic training at drill halls that were based in various large towns, these men also had to attend a, usually two week, summer camp.

Their style of numbering can cause confusion vis: 1/4, 2/4, 3/4, 1/5 and 2/5.

There is logic here as in the case of the 1/4: it is the fourth battalion, following on from the 3rd above; and the number one indicates it was the capable to serve alongside the regulars. When you see a 2 in front of the number this means it is a second line unit that were originally raised as reserve battalions for the first line which had volunteered for foreign service. A 3 means the less able through low numbers or age or possibly would have wounded men amongst its strength and were usually based permanently within the British Isles, again as a training unit.

Then came the six (Service) battalions of the Kitchener or New Armies. Initially formed of volunteers they were numbered 6 to 11, two of which like the 2 or 3/4 above were Reserve units, only to serve in the UK. The other four were trained to fight alongside the regulars; in fact the 7th (Service) Battalion DCLI contained the famous old soldier Harry Patch from Combe Down, Somerset, the so called 'Britain's Last Fighting Tommy' who died aged 111 on the 25th July 2009.

There were two more, the 12th Labour battalion that served on the Western Front and the 13th whose men did not see service within that unit as it was immediately absorbed into the Somerset Light Infantry.

As can be appreciated when projected throughout the whole army this amounts to an enormous number of men but ultimately nowhere near enough volunteers for a European land war. In 1914 the Regulars of the DCLI came from all over the UK, mainly from large towns and cities, the Territorials were initially at least mostly from the county and the Service battalions were a combination of both with preponderance to large urban centres somewhere in the UK. Many years ago I read that there were more men in the battalions that spoke with a Birmingham or East Midland accent than a Cornish one. An examination of the book for the *Soldiers who Died* when serving with the regiment supports this as the men were more likely to come from London, Birmingham and Northampton more often than Truro, Penzance or Bude.

Now at the end of this chapter we must acknowledge the fact that no less than 5,704,416 men, about a quarter of the adult male population of the United Kingdom, passed through the army during the war. Just under half, 2,446,719 were volunteers and the remainder were conscripted by one of the series of six Military Service Acts. These ever widened the pool from which to draw men into uniform, the first coming into force on the 27th January 1916[22].

The initial volunteers were trained in time for the 'Big Push' the battle that it was intended would break through the front and finish the war. However, although bravery was in abundance from officers and men alike, the Battle of the Somme [1st July to 18th November 1916] caused many deaths and terrible injury.

The battalions of Cornwall and Devon took their places in the line with the 1st, 2nd 8th and 9th Devons[23] being involved in the fighting at various stages and, if you visit the battlefield today, there is a 'Devonshire Cemetery' containing the graves of 161 men from the 8th and 9th Battalions. At its creation a carved wooden cross was erected, now replaced by a stone memorial bearing the same words *'The Devonshires Held This Trench, The Devonshires Hold It Still'*.

Also in combat were the 1st, 6th, 7th and the 10th & 12th (Pioneer) battalions of the Duke of Cornwall's Light Infantry[24]. If we take the 6th Battalion as a reference for the high casualty rates, between the 15th and 22nd of September at Flers-Courcelette 15 of their 20 officers and 294 soldiers out of 550 were killed or wounded.

During the Great War some 880,000 men died and this country records their sacrifice on various memorials in nearly every hamlet, village, town and city throughout the British Isles. What follows is a small statement of a part of their process marching on the long, long road to Armageddon. Whether survivor, volunteer or conscript their sacrifice or experiences should never be forgotten.

As two of six appendices I have included details of the four Cornishmen and four Devonians who were awarded the Victoria Cross during World War One. As this book it concentrates on the two counties all were born here and none served in either the DCLI or The Devonshire Regiment.

Although it is not within this books reemit it is to the pride of all who did serve in both regiments that there were soldiers who were awarded the VC, with many others receiving recognition for steadfastness and great bravery.

CHAPTER FOUR

Goodwill To All Men?

What led to this Great War and could it have been avoided? The answer is a qualified yes. Did the fictitious newspaper reports, books and articles raise tensions; this is a very qualified yes, as we have seen in these islands invasion scares had increased through 'popular' fiction. For example such publications as the1906 le Quex's book *The* [German] *Invasion of 1910* and the previously mentioned children's story *The Railway Children* drew attention to a message of perceived unpreparedness, plus weakness or subterfuge directed against Britain by 'an enemy' be it German, French, Russian or the 'dastardly traitor'. Indicative of its penetration of the British psyche le Quex's story serialised in *The Daily Mail* (above) under its Editor Alfred Harmsworth, had increased circulation. It has been calculated by 80,000 and in book form sold a million copies in 27 different languages[1]. We should acknowledge that in the German edition, obviously to guarantee sales, the Prussians won. Recognising a 'good thing when you see it' the same paper published an interview with a retired Prussian civil servant Rudolf Martin. He suggested *"In my judgment it would take two years for us to build motor-airships enough simultaneously to throw 350,000 men into Dover via Calais"* adding *"During the same night a second transport of 350,000 men could follow"*[2]. Although there were complaints in Parliament by MPs who argued that this type of literature potentially harmed our relationships with European powers in general and Germany in particular. They added that this may influence the British public to view a war with Germany as inevitable.

It was so influential that it later led to a government statement denying rumours that 66,000 German soldiers were resident in Britain. These men supposedly had access to a cache in central London containing 50,000 rifles and 7.5 million rounds of ammunition and who awaited the order to take over the country[3]. However, it was evident in the response to just one book that the theme would be pursued. As previously seen the increase in circulation brought about by such fiction rose by 80,000 but mainly in these counties bordering the North Sea as it cleverly focused on non-strategic locations which, cleverly, were named in the book[4]– what locals could resist. But, all would be well…of course:

London Evening Standard - <u>Monday 31 May 1909</u>

INVASION SCENE BY FIREWORKS. The football ground at the Crystal Palace, where so many great Cup finals have been fought out, is to be the scene of invasion drama of novel kind during the summer months, Messrs. Brock having to utilise the ground for the presentation of a 'firework-drama" every Thursday throughout the summer. The scenery is a thousand feet in length, and represents a peaceful English village. Territorials are seen drilling with newly invented gun which, it claimed, will put end to any likelihood of invasion by airships. A spy is captured, but escapes and signals to the enemy. Airships are then seen hovering around, and eventually foreign troops are landed, and a desperate fight ensues, involving the partial destruction of the village. The British troops emerge triumphant.

Putting fiction and wishful thinking aside, if we go back to the period 1899 – 1914, twenty Universal Peace Congress' were convened, the first with 300 delegates from Europe and the United States[5]. Its aims attracted those of high eminence in Britain and the United States, supported by vocal members of the general public and the clergy, who all brought pressure for the delegates to agree that that arbitration to avoid conflict should be sought. It was an achievable goal, as historically, between 1794 and 1914 this type of action did occur in over half of the 300 settlements that were eventually resolved after 1890. However, in Germany the peace movement did not have the support generated in other countries. With only about 10,000 active members drawn from the mainly the lower middle class, and, unlike Britain and the United States, amazingly the churches generally denounced it on the grounds that war was part of God's plan for mankind.

Times and circumstances change, so accordingly the common idea of disarmament later produced over 1,000,000 signatures from Germany with the document being sent to second Hague Peace Conference of 1907. But this had the qualification that *'We do not wish to disarm as long as the world around us bristles with bayonets'* adding the nationalist statement that the consequences must not diminish *"our position in the world"*. It must be added that the Kaiser was dismissive of such conferences stating that, although his country would attend, this was *"a comedy"* adding that he would *"keep his dagger by my side during the waltz"*. To underline this attitude one of his delegation included Karl von Stengel, who had written and published a pamphlet just before the proceedings started, condemning disarmament, arbitration and the whole peace movement.

In their defence, success and riches and their potential loss had even affected the minds of the British and we are an island nation. Although it may be difficult to recognise that militarism can disguise fear, if you go to Berlin or open an atlas, look eastwards over the excellent, mainly flat terrain. Then in your mind's eye imagine thousands of the enemy's cavalry sweeping down upon you.

What of the other Great Powers? Austria-Hungary whose peace movement was equally small generated little enthusiasm. Their Foreign Minister Goluchowski telling its delegates that *'we ourselves would scarcely wish that anything could be achieved'* and the French Foreign Minister Declasse did not want resolutions that indicated that his country must give up hope of peacefully regaining Alsace-Lorraine. Admiral 'Jacky' Fisher led Britain's delegates also little interest in disarmament, with the British Admiralty telling its government that a freeze on naval forces was *'quite impractical'*. Although Russia had seemed enthusiastic some nine years earlier, as the young Tsar it seems was partly motivated by idealism. But also his country was having trouble keeping up with the enormous expenditure of other European powers, relying on France for expertise and financial credit.

What of the United States? They had become a *de facto* imperial power since as we have seen they had smashed the power of Spain in both the western and eastern hemispheres. Acquiring Cuba and The Philippines in consequence, but at the start of the 20th century they still had a small army and navy compared to the major powers. It is with some cynicism that a French Admiral said to a delegate that *'they led the call for peace because they had destroyed the Spanish navy and commerce, and now wanted no one to destroy theirs'*. To sum up, the Belgian head of the commission correctly told his own government that no one was serious about disarmament[6].

There is nothing new however, in politicians 'spin':

North Devon Gazette - Tuesday 16 July 1907
THE PEACE CONFERENCE The Minister for Foreign Affairs, replying to journalists today, that contrary certain published statements, no difficulty existed regarding the deliberations of the Hague Conference. Very important agreements would be reached regarding the conditions of warfare.

Even with the above disdain for a reduction in weaponry and therefore a possible diminishing of tension and increased arbitration the outbreak of war was a shock. Simply put, the cause of the conflict would appear as if the Great Powers entered into the forthcoming catastrophe, not with a feeling of strength, but exactly the opposite from one of fear and their perceived weakness. The Austro-Hungarians, to regain their place as a first class power that they felt, correctly, they were losing, especially through the rise of internal nationalism. Germany, because it felt threatened and surrounded by France and Russia. The latter two because of the obvious burgeoning German military might; and Britain, because neutrality would make it vulnerable to the winner.

Some historians looking back towards the causes of the war, such as Annika Mombauer[7] have examined the fact that Britain's refusal to publicly pick a side prior to the conflict is important. She is of the opinion that this may have averted the war and possibly lifted the veil of suspicion surrounding the secret treaties of the first decade of the 20th century. She highlights that this belief existed at the time and was put forward by Germany as a fundamental cause of conflict. In 1914 for example, on July the 26th just 10 days before the declaration of war, King George V had expressed his opinion that Britain would remain neutral to his nephew Prince Henry of Prussia[8].

Western Daily Press - Monday 27 July 1914
Prince Henry of Prussia visited the King this morning. The King, the Queen, the Prince Wales, Princess Mary, and the ladies and gentlemen in attendance, were present at Divine Service in the private chapel this morning. Queen Alexandra, the Empress Marie Feodorovna

of Russia, the Princess Royal, Princess Victoria, Princess Maud and the Duke of Teck visited their Majesties, and remained to luncheon.

I support a little of this idea but with the proviso that contemporary observers thought German foreign policy was as capricious as it was aggressive[9] and as she herself noted on page 91 of her book. Helmuth von Moltke who became their new Chief of the General Staff was fully aware in 1911 that there was a strong chance 'England' would declare war if Belgium was invaded.

Ultimately it was Austria-Hungary and Germany who both decided, worse, gambled on military solutions that lead to a terrible catastrophe. Consequently British obfuscation and opaque foreign policy decisions can be seen to have, ultimately, played only a minor part.

As for the British Army, pre-war manoeuvres showed that it had made significant advances in professionalism and competence since the Boer War. Plans by the relatively newly established Staff College gave Lieutenant General James Grierson who was one of its central figures a guarded optimism. This seems to have abounded within the army in so much so that Colonel Richard Mienertzagen, a British officer of German decent, noted in his diary at the start of the war: *'Our Expeditionary Force is terribly small, but a mighty weapon, for every soldier can shoot and every man is determined to fight. The Germans will soon find that out. We are not the soldiers of the South African War'*[10]. However, he and all of the armed forces of the various protagonists were to soon discover that what had been planned and prepared for quickly unravelled. In the words attributed to Helmuth von Moltke [the elder] a previous Prussian Field Marshall and German Chief-of-Staff, when speaking of the Franco-Prussian War that *'No plan survives first contact with the enemy'*. This was definitely true for one soldier, as unfortunately the overweight and unfit James Grierson died of a heart attack just twelve days into the conflict on the 17th August 1914.

Duke of Cornwall's Rifle Volunteers

Boer War memorials, Exeter Cathedral

TO THE GLORIOUS MEMORY OF
TWO BROTHERS
CAPTAIN FRANCIS HUGH
SANDFORD D.S.O.
CROIX DE GUERRE AVEC PALMES
RN DARDANELLES DOVER PATROL
BORN 1887 DIED 1926
AND
LIEUT. RICHARD DOUGLAS
SANDFORD V.C.
LEGION OF HONOUR RN
SUBMARINE C.3 ZEEBRUGGE
BORN 1891 DIED 1918
SONS of ARCHDEACON SANDFORD of
EXETER
WHO IN A DARK HOUR OF PERIL
ON ST GEORGES DAY 1918
TOGETHER MAINTAINED THE
HIGHEST TRADITIONS OF THE NAVY

MAJOR GENERAL
C.W. PARK C.B.,
DIED 20TH MARCH 1913.
HE LED THE CHARGE OF THE
DEVONS ON WAGON HILL
6TH JANUARY 1900

IN MEMORY OF
THE UNDERMENTIONED N.C.OFFICERS & MEN
OF THE
73RD BATTERY ROYAL FIELD ARTILLERY
WHO LOST THEIR LIVES IN S. AFRICA DURING THE
BOER WAR 1899-1902

SERGEANT P. FORBES	GUNNER – W. GRIFFITHS	DRIVER – W. OLVER
Col. Hakr Serjt A. COOPER	,, J. GREGORY	,, F. BENNETT
CORPORAL H. MARSH	,, F. OXFORD	,, C. STEPHENS
Actg Bombr S. HAYES	,, W. WHITEBREAD	,, R. DEMPSTER
Shr Smith–C. SAWYER	,, W. BULL	,, J. TOMLINSON
H. JOHNSON	DRIVER – F. CALLARD	,, F. LONGMAN
GUNNER – J. TUCKER	,, B. CONSTABLE	,, W. HUGHES

ERECTED BY THEIR COMRADES.

CHAPTER FIVE

Semper Fidelis and One for All?

<u>**Exeter and Plymouth Gazette**</u> - <u>Monday 03 August 1914</u>
*SOCIALISTS S THE WAR DEMONSTRATION LONDON. united Labour and
Socialist demonstration, attended upwards of 20,000 people, took place in Trafalgar Square
yesterday afternoon protest against war. Mr Keir Hardie said the German workman had
war with the French and the French had no grievance against the Russian. They were told
that Treaty obligations compelled them to fight. The leading classes made the Treaties, and
workmen were led into war without having a say.*

For the justifiable reason of our preventing our involvement in a war involving Serbia,
Belgium, Russia and France against Germany and Austria-Hungary a crowd estimated at
20,000 gathered in Trafalgar Square, London. Most it is assumed supporting the left wing
politician and trade unionist Kier Hardy's call for peace. They all heard his statement that
'it was not the working man who made treaties to which the majority should abide but the 'leading classes'.
There was an echo of this sentiment in Cornwall when, far from a feeling of euphoria. The
Cornishmen newspaper soberly suggested: *If a referendum of the adults in the British Isles probably
not one in a hundred would vote for war.*

Of course there was not a referendum, neither was there a Parliamentary debate or division
as the decision was made by Royal Prerogative. Mind you although there were resignations
of ministers from the Cabinet there seemed little objection. On this unquestionably historic
day the House of Commons voted a credit of £100 million with barely a debate. Only
Ramsay Macdonald the leader of the Labour Party, with the agreement of his party, argued
for neutrality.

What of local opposition?

The British Neutrality Committee, with the names of Lord Courtney of Penwith
[Cornwall] and once again Mr. Ramsay Macdonald at the head of the signatories issued a
manifesto, declaring that we are not bound to be involved in a Continental war. In contrast
hand Macdonald was savagely attacked by the aggressive and arrogant Horatio Bottomly in
his ultra patriotic paper 'John Bull' writing that he was a traitor *'and that he be taken to the Tower*

and shot at dawn'. We had seen previously the pro-war crowd at Liskeard near rioting against Emily Hobhouse concerning the desperate situation of civilians in South Africa. Now eleven years later there was greater violence, this time at Plumstead Common, London. After the declaration on the 4th of August by the British Government condemning the German invasion of Belgium which violated the 1839 London Treaty stating the aggressors must retire. Anti-war protestors including Macdonald and members of the Independent Labour Party gathered at an anti-war rally. It is sad to say that they were attacked during fighting that erupted within the crowd, unfortunately this resulted with both the anti and pro-war attendees being injured, some carried away *'bleeding profusely'*.

Peace sadly, was not to be.

Exeter and Plymouth Gazette - Wednesday 05 August 1914
His Majesty's Government has declared t the German Government that a state war exists between Great Britain and Germany, from 11 p.m. August 4.

The Daily Mail Wednesday August 5th 1914
RUSH TO ARMS. MANY EX-SOLDIERS RE-ENLISTING.

It was back to the Army again at all the recruiting stations in the country yesterday. Recruiting sergeants had no need to go out to look for men: their only difficulty was repulsing those candidates who were more obviously unfit....

Did this rush continue, what happened after the *seeming* initial firework display of patriotism die away? Did the *Daily Mail* article reflect all of the provinces during the two years before the introduction of conscription and specifically, were there differences in the counties of Devon or Cornwall? Although Neville Erskin states that *'This enthusiasm and willingness to fight for one's country did not appear to wane, despite the enormous number of casualties that were faced by the British Forces'...*[1]. Is this wholly accurate? There has been little discussion of regional and class responses to the call that 'Your Country Needs You', blind obedience was not now a given and had obviously manifested itself in the major divisions that Edwardian society had previously faced[2].

In support of this 'war euphoria' we have all seen the newsreel of crowds in London, apparently large swirls of men caught in a celebratory mood trying to join the armed services after the declaration of war on the 5th August 1914. This was later summed up by Winston Churchill:

'It was 11 o'clock at night – 12 by German time – when the ultimatum expired. The windows of the Admiralty were thrown wide open in the warm night air. Under the roof from which Nelson had received his orders were gathered a small group of Admirals and Captains and a cluster of clerks, pencil in hand, waiting. Along the Mall from the direction of the Palace the sound of an immense concourse singing "God save the King" floated in[3].

War fever, the attitude that seemed to consume the British and by all accounts all the protagonists male and, on many occasions, females of the populations shouting 'On to Paris, On to Berlin, Death to the Kaiser, Plucky Little Belgium' indicating the readiness, the will to fight for their 'justified' cause. At the war's start there were long lines of recruits, in fact there were so many that initially the British authorities were overwhelmed the with young and not so young, educated and illiterate, fit but many who were definitely not, all trying to join the 'colours'. There are many books written at the end of the conflict that resonate with such sentiments. Amazon Kindle has Aubrey Smith's 'Four Years on the Western Front' reflecting his and his co-workers sentiments '...we went around to the Headquarters of the London Rifle Brigade and craved permission to enlist...' He does however end the sentence with ...in a manner that would have won the hearts of recruiting Sergeants in later days.

This early attitude could be attributed to many things, a desire for adventure, and a high degree of patriotism or group identity. Also, even that which amounted at times to a seeming blood lust[4] generated by probably previously good natured, decent and highly educated people showing just how enthusiastic for the conflict they were:

> If I were killed today, my chief regret,
> In this the greatest – worst of all the wars-
> Would surely be that I my fate had met
> Without a chance of furthering the cause.
>
> If I could one bullet in a foe
> Put just one German helmet in my kit,
> Then, if I have to, I am prepared to go
> For, after all, I've done my little bit.
> Lt. Alan Crawhall Challoner,
> 1/5 (Attached 'C' Co 6ᵗʰ (Service) Battalion.) DCLI.
> Educated St Paul's School, and Gonville and Caius College, Cambridge.
> Killed in Action 30ᵗʰ July 1915, Hooge, Ypres Salient, Belgium.

Prior to the introduction of Conscription, made law in January 1916 by Act of Parliament, there had been little inducement to join the purely volunteer armed services. Too many it was a place of last resort where the soldier or sailor could be clothed and fed, and therefore not relying on the capricious nature of employers or the workhouse. The army needed men but, as we have previously seen during the Boer War, many who attempted to join could not meet even the minimum standards the army required having suffered years of a poor diet and great physical hardship even when employed.

On the other hand in 1914 the Royal Navy initially had an excess of seamen as the number of smaller or outdated ships had been radically reduced by Admiral Lord Fisher's recent sweeping changes with the aim to create a new 'large gun' fleet. Britannia Ruled the Waves prior to 1914 and its then size now generated a lot of men in the reserves who were called once again to serve.

This issue had been recognised pre-war by the Admiralty and plans made that upon moblisation between 20 and 30 thousand men, without room on any ship of war, were to form elements of Marine and Naval Brigades to be used as infantry for home defence[5]. Therefore, and much to their initial displeasure, very quickly many hundreds of these reserve sailors were trained as infantry in the 63rd RN Division. This did not serve for home defence as envisaged but initially, as the manpower shortages were acute, on the Western Front as infantry.

Within the army, although the volunteer system was celebrated by most in the pre-war on both sides of the political arena, for various reasons including financial, it was decried by many in the armed services. They saw that it left Britain very vulnerable to large foreign armies with their thousands upon thousands of conscripts. These soldiers had a point.

Looking at the Western Front alone, the combatants in August and September 1914 in the German Army including Regulars, Reservists called up for duty and Landwehr (the older Reservists) amounted to approximately 1,485,000. Although Dennis Showalter questions many their individual effectiveness, stating they were *'less a people of warriors than a state of citizens in uniform*[6] their very size, as compared to our own British Expeditionary Force of 117,000[7] the old saying *'God favours the big battalions'* springs immediately to mind.

It should be noted that even the much smaller state of Belgians had 177,000[8] and France 1,071,000[9]. In fact the total number in the German Army was far bigger as they also fielded about another 200,000[10] on the Eastern Front. They needed them as they had immediately plunged themselves into a two front war and every man was required.

Now, a quick calculation shows that the Germans had around 120,000 more men on the Western Front than their enemies and possibly, more importantly, a unified command. They had planned for a quick war that produced a near repeat of the Franco Prussian just 43 years earlier. In their minds there was to be a minor, unopposed incursion of Belgium followed by a second capitulation of the French and gambled that Britain would not interfere.

But this did not happen and they consequently plunged the world into four long years of blood, tears, devastation and hatred. It must be immediately remembered that this Great War devoured people and places at a previously unknown rate. As quickly as volunteer units, e.g. such as our battalions of the Territorial Force were sent to the front they too were sucked into the maelstrom that by the end of 1914 resulted in the British Army alone suffering around 96,000 casualties. It has been estimated that by early 1915 there was only vestiges of the old army left[11].

Nationally, by early 1915 the recruitment numbers were not keeping pace with requirements. At a meeting of the War Cabinet on the 8th October Lord Kitchener pointed out that to maintain current numbers the army needed to recruit 35,000 *per week*[12], as the killed and wounded continued to rise. Something needed to be done.

In order to attempt to attain this number the best known of these above inducements was a regulation introduced in the same month. At that time Lord Derby was appointed Director-General of Recruiting and brought forward a process often named after him for raising the numbers of recruits, although its official title was the Group Scheme.

Men aged 18 to 40[13] were informed that under the scheme they could continue to enlist voluntarily or attest with an obligation to come if called up later on. The War Office notified the public that voluntary enlistment would soon cease and that the last day of registration would be 15 December 1915. On that date it was still estimated that some 600,000 men had still evaded enrolment, though, because of the appalling health of many within the working class population of those who had voluntarily enrolled or tried to enlist as volunteers, similarly to the Boer War, 50 percent were rejected as medically unfit[14].

Why would a man volunteer? In his book *The Last Great War. British Society and the First World War* Adrian Gregory states that several reasons can be examined for voluntary recruitment. The first is patriotism and the 'imperialist' sentiment of Britain before the war. The second is coercion, giving the shameful example of Bristol Poor Law Guardians who simply stopped paying relief to all 'able bodied' paupers in August 1914, 90 percent of whom, with little or no alternative tried to join the Army; and Lord Wemyss who threatened to sack and render homeless able-bodied labourers on his estates who didn't enlist. However, a more generous persuasion, or what may be termed 'bribery', occurred where employers pledged to pay or part-pay the volunteers whilst they were in the armed services. The bounty the men would receive in addition to any wages from the government, one such appeal being made by Lord Burnham at Beaconsfield who offered a one off payment of £10.00. Some were more generous, Leopold Salomons of Norbury Park offered his unmarried estate workers half pay and those married, full pay for the duration. Surrey County Council offered full pay, less that given by the army and guaranteed reinstatement at the end of hostilities plus an insurance scheme providing £100 to the family of those who died in service[15].

The Cornishman - Thursday 6th August 1914
Europe at War. Government votes 50 Million Sterling.

The major article on the front page deals at length with the reasons for the conflict and why the British Government had to take such a drastic step, noting that:

> *England cannot remain neutral without not only becoming isolated after the War but open to attack by which Power or Powers may emerge victorious from the titanic struggle.*

Although the paper does goes on to state our countries guarantees to Belgium and in fact this idea is today the general accepted logical reason why the British entered the war at all, the idea is also self serving. It contains within it also a realisation that we needed 'friends' as, unlike the Second World War, there were very few in Washington's White House who initially wanted to identify with or 'share the waves' with the British. All we could hope for was benevolent neutrality and the use of their latent manufacturing capacity. Professor Ian Beckett in '*The Victorians at War*' points out that Britain would be woefully underprepared for a continental war of any length. Post Boer War cutbacks in government arms production and leaving the manufacture of weapons and ammunition to the private sector led to shortages in its army in early 1915 with near catastrophic results. It was known at the time for example that in 1901 its factories were nearly two years behind in production and that orders for one month's supplies for the army were equivalent to what had been placed previously for twenty years. Unfortunately since the South African war ended before total mobilisation became necessary the lessons were not learned. On the other hand in its defence, the historian Spencer Jones in his *'From Boer War to World War'* touches on later criticisms of the relatively small size of the British Army as he writes that *'Yet it is important to remember that European militaries and governments all anticipated a short sharp war that would be over in a matter of months'* Given its perilous state during the retreat after the defeat at Mons and Kitcheners prediction of a three year war I suggest that some in the Army and government were actually praying for the war to be 'over by Christmas 1914'.

There were many who thought likewise as the cost of a long war would be insurmountable, those who did considered the financial implications: *Some think the war will be a short sharp one, costing each nation about one million* [pounds] *per day.* As Ian Senior writes, for completely different reasons, a confident Kaiser agreed. As they were about to leave for the front he promised his Prussian Guard that they would soon be victorious and would return 'before the leaves fell'.

A section of workers in Cornwall soon discovered how the war was to immediately affect them:

The Cornish Telegraph - Thursday 6th August 1914
A thousand Cornish china clay workers are under a weeks' notice.

A week later:

Events on the Continent obviously covered many column inches: *Germany Invades Belgium. The British Foreign Office was informed by the Belgian Minister that German troops had crossed into Belgium.*

It has long been acknowledged that disagreement in the cabinet between the doves and hawks could have split the Government and led to its fall. In fact several Ministers did resign but as Bourne puts it *'there seemed no other realistic choice, after the Germans had obligingly violated Belgium neutrality'.*

St Austell Star - Thursday 6th August 1914
Reported on the statement to the House of Commons.

He assured the House that in the current crisis, up until Sunday, the Government had given no promise to any country of anything more than diplomatic support.

He was being 'economical with the truth' as certain assurances had been made with France and a rapprochement made with Russia. Unfortunately this latter conversation or, as some put it *'an entente too far'* limited even further Britain's room for manoeuvre in the July and August crisis.

The military plans for possible involvement on the Continent [The War Book] written by the arch Francophile General Henry Wilson, were extensive and put immediately put into action. The army were beaten to it by Winston Churchill who, on the 27th July 1914 confirmed the order of the First Sea Lord, Prince Louis of Battenberg that the fleet should not disperse after its concentration for a Spithead Review, but instead proceed to its war stations.

In North Devon the populace was made aware of the German invasion and the appeal by the Belgians to the British Government. The below is a literal translation of a telegram read to the Commons by Asquith the Prime Minister:

North Devon Journal - Thursday 06 August
I regret to have to inform his Majesty's Government that this morning the armed forces of Germany penetrated territory in violation of her engagements assured by treaty. The Belgian Government are firmly resolved to resist by all means in their power. Belgium appeals to Great Britain, France and Russia to co-operate as guarantors in defence of her territory and that their concerted and common action with the object resisting the forcible measures employed by Germany against Belgium.

St Austell Star - Thursday 6th August 1914
A very large number of Mevigissey men have been or still are in the Naval Reserve. The ringing of the bell by the town-crier and the call to reservists to turn out, was the first intimation of the news….Many men had been expecting the call after the declaration of war the previous day… but in an incredibly short time everyone was astir, some even in reserve costume.

But the thoughts and feelings of their relations appeared a different matter …...for although the reservists themselves were so cheerful, those who were left behind could not help think of what might happen before the gallant little band came home again, or whether they would all come back.

The Cornish Telegraph - Thursday 6th August 1914
About 156 Reservists left Penzance on a special train Sunday afternoon. Others will follow.

Cornish Guardian - Friday 7th August 1914
FOWEY ROYAL NAVAL RESERVES.

A good deal of excitement occurred Fowey and Polruan on Sunday, when it became known that the order had been sent to all the Naval Reserve. Over a hundred Petty Officers and men surrendered at once for service and were conveyed brakes (motor vehicles) etc to Par station.

Exeter and Plymouth Gazette - Saturday 08 August 1914
AN APPEAL TO PATRIOTIC DEVONIANS. Exeter, during the past few days, has become accustomed the march of troops through her streets, but yesterday she witnessed a sight which must have thrilled the most apathetic her citizens and touched patriotic chord in the hearts of even the most stoical of her sons and daughters. The occasion was the through

the city the Reservists of the County's own regiment——the Devons—who. in the last have bought glory and renown to their native county, and assisted in small degree assure the success England's arms all parts of the world. The object of the march was to attract recruits to the colours, remind Devon's young men where lay their duty during these days of our Empire's trials. England needs men to defend the right against the aggressor, and it was felt that Devon, with all her glorious records, required but the word for her respond one man the call to arms which is now sounding throughout the Empire

Exeter had been quick to recognise hording could be a problem and had taken steps to avoid it, plus providing medical support for those 'called to the colours':

Exeter and Plymouth Gazette - Wednesday 12 August 1914
...doctors in the town had offered to attend free necessitous cases of families of soldiers and sailors at the war, that the chemists the town had offered to prepare doctors prescriptions in such case at cost price, and that grocers, provision dealers, bakers, and confectioners had agreed supply only the average weekly orders their customers.

The Cornish Telegraph - Thursday 13th August 1914
About 80 men were discharged from the Belkin Mine, St. Just, on Saturday.

This not only shows that unfortunately 'zero hours' contracts are obviously not a new thing but also the, unforeseen by many, consequences of war time.

The Cornishman - Thursday 13 August 1914
Lord Kitchener's appeal, recruits for the Regular Army are flocking to the standard.......

The Cornish Telegraph - Thursday 13 August 1914
WEST CORNWALL NEWS.

Early on Monday morning, fourteen St. Ives Royal Naval Reservists returned from the Irish herring fishery, motored to St. Erth, and trained for Devonport.

Four more naval reservists have left for active service. Some of those who left previously will join the Lusitania for transport services.

Unfortunately in times of crisis many look after themselves first, with the unconscious (?) attitude of "Let the devil take the hindmost 'as in the same edition:

Councilor Lethby has given notice of the following motion for the Council meeting on Wednesday next: "This Council authorizes the Mayor their behalf to issue an appeal to the wealthier inhabitants not to buy up large stocks of the necessities of life, and regrets that some tradesmen are charging excessive prices for certain articles of food which bears heavily upon the poor of the town."

St. Austell Star - Thursday 20th August 1914
NAVAL INFORMATION BUREAU FOR FOWEY AND DISTRICT.

Notice to Relatives and Officers and Men of Royal Naval Marines (who are on active service.) An Information Bureau been opened in Fowey which will be in direct communication with the Special Information Bureau opened in our large naval ports and elsewhere….and relatives wanting any help or advice are asked to apply to the Fowey bureau, rather than write to the Admiralty or elsewhere in London.

Brixham, a large fishing town besides providing men for the RNR was also pleaded with for men to serve in the army. Unquestionably it was now coming home to the government just how many men were required.

Brixham Western Guardian - Thursday 20 August 1914
They must however, have soldiers, because they had not enough for a struggle of such immense magnitude. They should provide the men to-day who with a few months' training, would be able to get in the second blow, and provide the German Emperor with his Waterloo-- (hear. hear)

As its name suggests Mousehole was a tiny fishing village so the below would have had immediate and far reaching effects:

The Cornish Telegraph - Thursday 20 August 1914
Upwards of 10 fishermen attended a meeting Mousehole on Friday evening, Mr. Tregenza presiding. Mr. Stephen Reynolds was informed there were 78 Royal Naval Reserve men gone from the town representing over 40 families.

The following shows the number required each unit of the Cornwall Territorial Force: Squadron, Royal Ist Devon Yeomanry. No vacancies; Garrison companies. 19 men required; Cornwall R.E., no vacancies; 4th D.C.L.1., men required; 5th D.C.L.1., 200 men required.

St. Austell Star - Thursday 20th August 1914
SOLDIERS' WIVES AND FAMILIES. SEPARATION ALLOWANCES For general information the War the following notification respecting the separation allowance for wives and children of soldiers, mobilised Reservists (including Special Reservists), members of the Territorial Force called up for active service, and civilians enlisted for temporary service daring war….

I think it safe to say that those men committed by previous service whether in the army or navy honoured their contractual agreement and duly joined their units. That the state had guaranteed financial support for their families must have added to the peace of mind to those going off to war. Seemingly, there seems to have been a feeling of understanding and acceptance on behalf of their relatives.

The news of the first battle involving the heavily outnumbered BEF against the German 1st Army of *Alexander von Kluck* was at this stage of the conflict slow in reaching the provinces.

Cornishman - Thursday 27th August 1914
British Forces Engaged Holding their own at Mons

The Official Press Burian (sic) announces that the British forces were engaged all day and after dark with the enemy in the neighbourhoid (sic) of Mons and held their ground. No information has been received regarding casualties, which will be published once known.

The Cornish Telegraph – also dated the same day and again a Penzance paper unsurprisingly reports the same but also has an article indicating that the war may be a long one: *COUNTY OF CORNWALL PATRIOTIC Patron. H.R. THE PRINCE OF WALES. SUBSCRIPTIONS are invited to the above Fund and may paid to the Mayor of any Borough, the Chairman of any Urban or Rural District Council, the Chairman of the Council of the Isles of Scrlly (sic), or to the Hon. Treasurer, Barclay and Co., Truro, or any Bank.*

Now the papers begin to receive news of the actual fighting which makes interesting reading in comparison to what actually happened. It is also far more martial, aggressive and to the modern era, vainglorious in tone. We also see the first use of disingenuous 'spin':

St Austell Star - Thursday 3rd September
OUR DAYS' BATTLE. BRITISH ARMY'S GLORIOUS ACHIEVEMENTS. ENEMY FOUGHT TO A STANDSTILL HEAVY BRITISH LOSSES. On Sunday afternoon the following was communicated by the Secretary of State for War. Although the official dispatches from Sir John French on the recent battles have not yet been received, it is possible now to state in general outline what the British share in the recent operations has been. There has in effect been a four days' battle, on August 23, 24, 25, and 26. During German attack, which was stubbornly pressed and repeated. However, it was completely checked on the British front. the whole of this period the British troops, in conformity with the general movement of the French armies, were occupied in resisting and checking the German advance and in withdrawing to the new lines of defence. The battle – began at Mons on Sunday, during which day and part of the night, the (sic) continues….

On Monday, August 24, the Germans made vigorous efforts in superior numbers to prevent the safe withdrawal of the British Army and to drive it into the fortress of Maubeuge. The effort was frustrated by the steadiness and skill with which the British retirement was conducted, and, as on the previous day, very heavy losses, far in excess of anything suffered by us, were inflicted upon the enemy, who in dense formation and in enormous masses marched forward again and yet again to storm the British lines.

DESPERATE FIGHTING. The British retirement on August 25 with continuous though not on the scale of the previous two days and by the night of August 25 the British Army occupied the line Cambrai-Landrecies-Le Cateau. It had been intended to resume the retirement at daybreak on August 26, but the German attack, in which no less than corps were engaged, was so close and fierce that it was not possible to carry out this intention until the afternoon. The battle of this day was of most severe and desperate character. The troops offered a superb and most resistance to the tremendous odds with which they were confronted and at length extricated themselves in good order though with serious losses and under heaviest artillery fire. No guns were taken by the enemy except those the horses of which were all killed, or which were shattered by high explosive shells. Sir John French estimates that during the whole of these operations from August 23 to August 26 inclusive his looses amount to 5,000 or 6,000 men.

It adds

On the other hand the losses suffered by the Germans in their attacks through their dense formations are out of all proportion to ours.

The basic facts are correct. However, the Battle of Mons took place on the 23rd August. The Germans won the battle and, because of the size of their forces, ensured a complete and immediate retreat by both British corps as ordered by its commander General Sir John French. The casualties suffered by the British in this one day battle amounted to 1638[16] men, the Germans an estimated 2,000, not quite the *'very heavy losses, far in excess of anything suffered by us, were inflicted upon the enemy'*. Consequently there never was a fully manned Cambrai-Landrecies- Le Cateau- Line and the enemy were never *'completely checked on the British front'*.

In fact both corps retreated south either side of the densely wooded Forest of Mormal. The 1st Corps, under General Sir Douglas Haig to the eastern side and 2nd Corps, commanded by the newly appointed General Sir Horace Smith Dorian, on its western edge. Although the plan intended a steady, controlled withdrawal in parallel with one another, the situation soon became confused. Battle was often joined with the pursuing Germans forces that at times, threatened total disintegration.

2nd Corps fought two delaying actions on the 24th at Frameries and Audregnies and another at Elouges that frustrated von Kluck's attempt at envelopment. Although successful in preventing total defeat, it was at the terrible cost of nearly 5,000 casualties, including nearly all of the 1st Battalion of the Cheshire Regiment. It should be remembered that the infantrymen of the German 1st Army had been on foot since entering Belgium. Quite possibly tiredness and inexperience, plus the shooting skills of the British, led to the Germans losing an estimated 15,000 men during these battles, some three times greater[17].

The next day saw a serious rearguard action at Landrieces for 1st Corps and rearguard skirmishes at Solesmes for 2nd Corps[18] that created a very serious situation for Smith-Dorian. 'Death by a thousand cuts' or stand and fight wishing and hoping to damage the Germans enough to make him pause in his offensive actions and regroup. Smith-Dorian took the courageous act to disregard French's retreat orders. This was permissible as Field Service Regulations permitted the 'man on the spot', to stand and fight and he chose to do so at the town of Le Cateau on the 26th with about 60,000 men[19]. Most historians of the period agree that this was needed to stop the possible disintegration of 2nd Corps [plus the newly arrived 4th Division] as they were under relentless German pressure. Although not 'smashing' the enemy as some have claimed, the battle's result was as hoped for as it allowed the British to continue its, at times, desperate retreat. But ultimately British losses were high with around 7,812[20] infantry casualties that include 2,500 made prisoners, plus the loss of 38 artillery pieces. The Germans suffered an estimated 2,000 casualties.[21]. Therefore, allowing for the confusion of battle the actual events as reported are surprisingly accurate.

Although the British were able to disengage its casualties between the 24th and 26th were appalling and far greater than that reported in their newspapers. Modern scholarship shows the BEF as a whole lost 14,126 men against a German total of 4,000. Shocking indeed but logical when you consider the British were retreating and a fighting rearguard actions against a far stronger enemy. Although 1st Corps were not involved in such a major battle during the retreat, it too fought several smaller actions against its pursuers. To note is that one unforeseen benefit was gained: because the BEF had split into two disparate blocks this caused confusion, slowing and sowing uncertainty in the German advance.

It has recently been stated that the Germans lost the war on the 23rd August 1914 because of faulty recognisance by their cavalry. The British were not 'on the run', they couldn't, but they were retreating as fast as their exhausted legs could carry them; and the French armies' left wing was hanging 'in the air' open to total envelopment. The Germans possessed overwhelming force but confusion and exhaustion ultimately led to a protracted, unforeseen war. Such is conflict where chance plays a part and mistakes by an enemy allow victory sometimes more that decisions taken by your own side.

See: *Chasing the Retreat. The German Cavalry Pursuit of the British Expeditionary Force before the Battle of the Marne August 1914.* Authors: Declercq, Gilbert and Robinson.

What of the DCLI? They were fortunate at Mons being on the extreme left of the line and not engaged in any great action during the battle. At Le Cateau they were now on the extreme right of the line with the 1st East Surrey battalion. Because of the rapid decisions being taken they did not receive orders to stand and fight, but to continue the retreat at 0630 (6.30am). Unfortunately while forming up, they were attacked by lead elements of German Infantry Regiment 72. Recovering from the initial surprise, the column fought its way down the valley to rejoin 14th Brigade at Honnchey aided by some very effective fire from L Battery RHA [Royal Horse Artillery][22]. Nevertheless, they suffered around 200 casualties….

The Cornishman - Thursday 10th September 1914
PENZANCE NATIONAL RESERVE DISTRICT. The following returns of recruits for the week ending September 5th 1914… Regular Army 10, Territorials 26, Yeomanry 5, total, 41. The totals to-date are: Regular, 22, Territorials 78, Yeomanry 5, total, 105. These figures include ten men from the Isles of Scilly.

In the same edition: *At Cardiff recruits numbered nearly 7,006.*

What do these numbers indicate? Given the seeming lack of enthusiasm with only 10 men signing up for the Regular Army I think we can certainly postulate that the 26 who became members of the Territorials did not agree to sign for Imperial Service i.e. to serve abroad if called upon to do so. Those for the yeomanry may be seen as a wish to join, in their and Edwardian society's mind, a better 'class' of person. Three of such are named: *RECRUITS FROM PENZANCE Recruits enlisted for Devon Yeomanry include Messrs. C. E. Venning, B. B. Bennetts, and Walter J. Pool.* - Vennings and Bennetts companies were and are solicitors in Penzance; Pool came from a Hayle based wealthy engineering family. B.B. Bennets later became an officer in a Highland regiment. He probably used the status of the yeomanry to promote his suitability as an officer; a somewhat similar route as taken by Siegfried Sassoon [23]. Surprising as it may appear today it was not that unusual at the time. For example the 69th Naval Division had advertised for 'suitable men' [to become officers] and many were appointed after an informal interview. What was the criterion for the appointment? For some it was service as an officer in the Merchant Navy, or previous managerial experience, this being ever so tenuous in some cases. But most for reasons we can only guess: possibly the right school, accent, or clothing, even golf club membership[24].

The Cornish Telegraph - Thursday 10th September 1914
LORD KITCHENER'S ARMY. 20,000 BIRMINGHAM RECRUITS.

There was a great increase in recruiting Birmingham Monday, very large numbers of men presenting themselves it was estimated that at least 20,000 men have joined Lord Kitchener's army, either as ordinary recruits or in companies of professional or non-manual workers. Many of the larger employers of labour are discharging men between the ages of twenty and thirty-five, and are replacing them with older men obtained through the Labour Exchanges.

ENTHUSIASTIC SEND OFF. About 270 men have gone, from the St Ives, including the Naval Reserve, 61 Territorials, 11 National Reservists, 5 Yeomanry, 4 K.G.A. etc. Two hundred and seventy out of 7,000…..

However, there were complaints in both counties that many were not doing as expected. In early September the editor of The Trewman's Flying Post wrote that *'There are some Little Englanders in Topsham who from fear of losing their work or of saving their lives still hold aloof from doing their duty to the Old Country'.*

The Cornishman - Thursday 24th September 1914
PATRIOTIC MEETING AT GOLDSITHNEY. Never in the history of Goldsithney has a meeting been more largely attended than was the patriotic meeting held on Tuesday evening…. Previous to the speeches Mr. Stanley Smith played patriotic airs, and Mr Jasper (Penzance) sang -Rule Britannia," he being accompanied on the piano by Mr. E.

Tregarthen. Capt. J. J. Henderson, recruiting officer, explained the recruiting movement, and begged them consider it in a serious light.

The war he thought *would be long duration, and every man would be wanted those times of strife, lie himself was going to the front* (Applause)…..referring to the remarks which had been made which reflected on the courage of Cornishmen because such a large number had not enlisted in the Army, Capt. Henderson said it could be accounted for by the fact that by far the greater number joined the Navy.

Mr. J. A. Hawke, K.C., prospective Unionist candidate for the St. Ives division… *"speaking as a Cornishman"* he said *"he knew that Cornishmen took little while to consider things before taking action, and therefore, he did not expect to see them all rushing to enlist at the first moment. Cornwall was not backward in patriotism"*. Captain Hudson then called for recruits, but there was no response. This must have something of a shock, but he did have a point about naval enlistment. As we have seen naval reservists when called upon went off to war in great numbers a fact very well known to this unresponsive audience.

The figures below illustrate that there were wide differences during this early stage in the conflict and confirm the rush to enlist seen in many areas of the country.

North Devon Journal - Thursday 24 September 1914
NEW ARMY RECRUITS AT BARNSTAPLE. to date, Sergeant major Dannis, the recruiting officer for the Barnstaple district has enrolled 160 men towards one million asked for by Lord Kitchener far His Majesty's Army.

As for the Territorials: Lord Kitchener as the newly appointed Secretary of State for War had decided that whole divisions of the Territorial Force should be sent to India[such as the Wessex division]. These would replace the more experienced 'regular' units so that they could return to fight in France. This of course only applied to those men who, as part-time soldiers, had signed the Imperial Service Obligation..

Cornish Guardian - Friday 02 October 1914
BODMIN "TERRIERS" FOR INDIA. Recently we gave a list of the names of the Bodmin Territorials who have volunteered for foreign service and in the course of a few days in company with their regiment, the 4th battalion and other men of the Territorial Army, they will proceed to India to undertake garrison duty and to relieve regular troops for service with the Expeditionary Force. The members of the Battalion have been allowed short leave prior to sailing.

To replace these foreign-service units, the Territorial Force was doubled in size by creating a second line which mirrored the organisation of the original, first-line units. Second-line units assumed responsibility for home defence and provided replacement drafts to the first line. The second line competed with the New Army for limited resources and was poorly equipped and armed. For example such were the shortages during the early stages of the war that many units had their Lee Enfield rifles substituted by old Japanese Arisaka rifles as the originals were needed at the front.

Service in the RN and Merchant Navy

This shows that the casualties suffered in Devon and Cornwall by its Royal Marine and Naval personnel were nearly four times that of the national average

Service/Town or village	Royal Navy	Merchant Marine	Army	Unknown
Appledore	11	32	30	
Beer	6		17	1
Braunton	5	2	33	
Cullompton	3		68	
Bideford	11		171	
Torrington	6		51	
St Ives	14	4	75	18
Mevagissy	17		27	
Newlyn	20	6	15	
Newquay	7	8	84	28
Total	100	52	571	47
UK Deaths totals	32287	15000	744000	

DEVON and CONWALL Total	770			
RN and merchant total	152			
Total Army	618	inc. Unknown		
Percent of RN and MM in comparison to the Army	24.59			

NATIONAL Total	791287			
RN and merchant total	47287			
Total Army	744000			
Percent of RN and MM in comparison to the Army	6.35			

In 1916, referring to Cornwall, a correspondent to *The Times* wrote that: *When the Navy first made ready for the War (sic), nearly 600 men left the county on one Sunday evening, and it is said that as many as 300 followed them the next day. Three hundred went from St Ives district alone. These were naval reservists, and they are now at sea….The draining of men has goner steadily on until in many places only one third of the original male fishing population is left to man the boats.*

Likewise at Brixham in Devon the *Fishing News* reported on the 8th August 1914, that over 200 men had been called up to serve in the Royal Naval Reserve. Douglas D'Enno in his book *'Fishermen Against the Kaiser'* states that Plymouth with its smaller fleet lost 80 to the RNR and 20 to the dockyard. Many memorials to the deceased do not list the service in which the deaths occurred. I have found ten that did - four in Cornwall and six in Devon. I write this with the greatest respect because, as individuals, these fishermen were not a statistic. In Devon and Cornwall by the end of the war their pre-war numbers had shrunk by 24.5 percent, loses that are comparable to those suffered in either the Royal Navy or the civilian Merchant Navy.

Now after two months after the declaration of war and increased unemployment it is obvious that many of the previously employed [China] clay workers had been laid off and therefore one would have thought more likely to enlist. However some two months later:

Cornish Guardian - Friday 2nd October 1914
..one may take it for granted that in the opinion of those in a position to judge, recruiting in Cornwall generally, and the clay district specifically has not been up to expectations....

The tone of the article, written anonymously by "Observer" is censorious, praising those who have enlisted but goes on to state: *Let the laggard realize at once that Cornwall is not doing so well as she might or ought, despite the apologists.....and only brisk recruiting for the next few weeks can save the Delectable Duchy from the reproach of slackness.*

The article goes on to write about and then quote from the recruiting speech given by a local eminent Edwardian, Sir Arthur Quiller-Couch. He was a scion of two famed local families, an intellectual, plus active in local politics for the Liberal Party and author of the *Oxford Book of English Verse, 1250–1900.* The main aim of the address was in an attempt to recruit a million men, saying the powerful effect this may have *...even if they are never in the firing line....*

The tone of the report would indicate either patriotic naivety on his part at best, or possible disingenuousness, as this was written while the DCLI was fighting at the Battle of the Aisne of September 1914. It was during this offensive that the BEF sustained another 5000 casualties, having already been involved in the battles of Mons and Le Cateau.

"This is the point" said Sir Arthur *"that from the moment you enlist you are helping the man in the trench. At the moment of enlisting you are relieving another trained man, to take his place or stand by his side while you are preparing yourselves."*

It would be wrong to ascribe him as being a hypocrite, expecting others to do what he at aged 50 could not, nor as an uncaring 'toff' as he had chaired the meeting in Liskeard when Emily Hobhouse had attempted to speak about the conditions in the British Concentration Camps. In fact he was instrumental in raising, at Truro, the 10th Battalion the DCLI (Pioneers) and whose son [Oxford] OTC trained and Special Reservist, Major Bevill Quiller-Couch MC served continuously from Mons 1914 to November 1918 on the Western Front in the Royal Field Artillery[25]. Because of this however, his father was in a position to know what was happening so was he unconsciously showing special interest, hoping large numbers of recruits would ease the dreadful burden on his son and comrades? We will never know[26].

In two other examples of 'noblesse oblige' Captain Tommy Agar-Robartes, Coldstream Guards of Lanhydrock House died while trying to rescue a wounded man on 30th September 1915 for which action he was recommended for the VC. And Edward (later Sir Edward) Bolitho of Trengwainton House, a regular officer in the Royal Artillery, who served from 1900, was awarded the DSO.

What of Devon, although the below points out the majority of men who had enlisted were from the county, that six counties produced 88 is nowhere near those who were needed.

Western Times - Friday 23rd October 1914

Recruits for Kitchener's Army coming steadily. On Wednesday 88 were enrolled in No. 8 Military District as follows: Devon (Exeter) 31 Somerset 13 Cornwall 7 Hants 25 Dorset 2 Wilts 10.

The same Devon paper on the next day, below, reported that the numbers nationally were not that required to fill the rapidly depleting ranks. Initially, because of a glut in recruiting, the standards had been raised, this was now reversed and the physical abilities to serve were lowered:

Western Times - Saturday 24th October 1914

MORE MEN Urgently Needed for Kitchener's Armies. It is stated that about 300,000 more men are needed to complete the million men for Kitchener's new armies, about 700,000 having already enlisted. A new proclamation was issued on Thursday asking for additional men at once, to complete the "second half million and ensure success abroad and safety at home." Standards for recruiting have been lowered, as follows: Height, 5 feet 4 inches (down to normal); age, 19 to 38 (increase three years); old soldiers up to 45. Ex-non-commissioned officers are still required for abroad. The recruiting authorities state that every available man is wanted urgently. An Army Order was issued on Thursday, stating that the King has approved the payment of a special recruiting reward of one shilling in respect of each recruit enlisted for the Army for the period of the present war.

On the 3rd of November 1914 the first of several attacks were made against mainland British towns by the Imperial German Navy. The assault was made against Great Yarmouth, a pre-war popular seaside resort, by a group of naval craft of eight cruisers led by Admiral Hipper in SMS Seydlitz. [SMS: Seiner Majestät Schiff", or "His Majesty's Ship" in German]

The weather conditions were poor with a heavy mist. Consequently the action that followed the ships being spotted and engaged with gunfire by a patrolling RN minesweeper HMS Halcyon appeared less than spectacular. Completely outgunned, Halcyon incurred injuries and damage forcing it to withdraw. Following this Admiral Hipper then ordered shelling to commence against the town. They all missed. After a short time and concerned that they could be intercepted by a much larger British force, the German forces then departed.

Although it has been written *'While it came as a shock to residents all along the east coast that German ships could carry out such an operation...'* local newspapers made light of the matter[27]:

Yarmouth Independent - Saturday 07 November 1914
YARMOUTH SHELLED ? The answer to this question must an emphatic -Yes! Had people for a moment imagined that the German guns blazing away out of the morning mist east of the Cross Sand, were potting at Yarmouth they would not have lined the Parade as they did to witness the performance. They remained in blissful ignorance, and fortunately our enemy's shells did not reach the town. What had no doubt happened was that German cruiser squadron, slipping out of port during the night, had got within a few miles of the English coast, to lay mines. It was met by the little British fishery protection cruiser Halcyon, which promptly and pluckily fired at the big warships. Their marksmanship "made in Germany," proved to be, as usual, indifferent, but they hit the Halcyon two three times, and wounded one her crew. A long one-sided running fight ensued, but the small British craft got away. Thus far the raiders had spent a good deal of powder and shot with very small effect. Their bombardment of Yarmouth was even less effective.

Surprisingly on the same date in Devon a report seemed to actually discount that such an action had even taken place:

Western Times - Saturday 07 November 1914
MUST WE BELIEVE IT? The German Headquarters to-day issued report to the effect that November 3rd large and small cruisers attacked the British coast, off Yarmouth, and shelled the works and vessels anchored. The British forces which protect this important port were not then there.

The attack on Great Yarmouth seems to have been ranked of low importance to the government. Possibly because it took place around the time of the Battle of Coronel, in the Pacific off the coast of Chile against the German Pacific fleet. This the British decidedly lost, so could it be that they didn't want the public thinking its 'Senior Service' wasn't up to either sinking German ships or protecting its home shores?

These battle reports certainly didn't create a rush to join the armed services; but one possible idea was put forward, a healthier lifestyle as an inducement to volunteering.

The Cornishman - Thursday 12th November 1914
A Cornish lady, who is in close touch with members of 2,000 troops at a Cornish resort, tells us that many of them previous to joining the force had been rather troubled with weakness of the chest lungs. Since joining they have improved in health in every way. She thinks if this were widely known it should greatly stimulate recruiting, as there are many people in Cornwall delicate health, who would benefit from the open-air life.

The below is very interesting and I discus it below the press report.

Western Times - Friday 20 November 1914

DEVON RECRUITING Army Officer Says the Farmers are holding men back. An Army officer occupying a important position in No. 8 District voiced his opinion this week that the young men in Devon were not coming forward for Kitchener's Army in the way they might. He believed he said that farmers were keeping men by putting difficulties the way of their joining. Not enough farmers' sons were enlisting. August Devonians came forward well, but since the reversion like lower standard the lull had been pronounced! Cornwall was now showing as good better returns than Devon. Devon, he considered, was as far from being played out as yet. When reminded that the Territorial units wore enrolling many men, and that this was undoubtedly affecting recruiting for Kitchener's Army, the officer agreed, but insisted that it was more important that the Regular Army should added to. The Reserve Territorial regiments could wait for time. He then pointed to Hull as a town that had set a good example in the matter of recruiting. Hull had a very large proportion of young men had come to the colours. But Hull was on the East coast, and the population were thoroughly alive to the dangers invasion. "People down here I suppose won't realise the danger of the country they see hostile airships or something that sort."

The above is a very interesting article that touches on several apparent issues for a lack of recruits in Devon at this stage of the war. Were farmers holding their men back, especially their sons? Also by now with inflation and the reduction of foodstuffs compared to pre-war supplies, this could be seen that all workers were required to work the land. When mentioning Cornwall, who had not provided large numbers of recruits, it is obvious he was touching on county rivalry.

The recruitment campaigns were aimed at men to serve wherever it was decided to send them. But joining the Territorials at this time still gave soldiers the option of electing for Home Service only. Comparing Devon to Hull, Yorkshire also illustrates that he contended 'out of sight meant out of mind' applied when it came to the vagaries of combat. However, events during the next month brought events in the north-east to the forefront of any British appreciation of the naval war.

In the mean time what was happening in France and Belgium? After the German advance through Belgium and eastern France this was curtailed by a decisive Allied victory in the Battle of the Marne in late September 1914. Thus began the so-called "Race to the Sea", as each army attempted to outflank the other so, ensuring the conflict moved northwards. For the British the race ended in mid-October at Ypres, the ancient, historic and beautiful Flemish city in the west of Belgium famous for its Cloth Hall. Ultimately of course, the newly established line reached the last open area from Diksmuide to the North Sea which was occupied by Belgian troops.

The troops of the BEF, still commanded by Sir John French, arrived in the Ypres area between October the 8th and 19th to reinforce the existing Belgian and French defenders. Meanwhile, the new German Chief of Staff, Erich von Falkenhayn, prepared to launch the first phase of an offensive aimed at breaking the Allied lines, capturing Ypres and the Channel Ports. On October 19, a protracted period of fierce combat began as the Germans opened their Flanders offensive that the Allies steadfastly resisted. The fighting continued with heavy losses on both sides until November 22 when high casualties and the arrival of winter weather convinced the Germans to halt the offensive, bringing the battle to a halt. The area between the positions established by both sides during this period—from Ypres on the British side to Menin and Roulers on the German side—became known as the Ypres Salient, a region that over the course of the next several years would see some of the war's bitterest and most brutal struggles. For the British it had been an extremely close run encounter with the line on many occasions being near to breaking. However, although they held on to the city this event is considered to be the 'Death of the old BEF/British regular Army' having suffered around 58,000 casualties. The remainder were desperate for trained reinforcements.

Unfortunately in the West Country a month later, statistics still showed the overall lack of enthusiasm:

> **St Austell Star** - Thursday 26th November 1914 and **The Cornish Guardian** – Friday 27th November 1914
>
> *In a Celtic race like the Cornish (of which we may presume seventy percent per are Celts) an appeal to enlist their sympathies or themselves be a wordy lecture or letter is not likely to be productive of much good. Facts have already justified this assertion in this neighbourhood, where, after a series of stirring patriotic speeches, the meetings have ended without scrolling a single recruit for the nations needs.*

The writer, a local man, goes on to assert the reason being that the Cornish were not used to seeing the military man, stepping out to martial airs and things would change: *Show them the brave, stirring life, and let them hear the appealing music of the regiments, and Cornishmen would make a far better return of enlistments than are now dragging in….*

As…..*Cornwall has is its sturdy youth rare material for the making of good soldiers, as they are so inured to headships by their labours in the clay pits in all weathers, in mines quarries, in the fields; but the fact remains our youth have been out of touch with the soldier's life…..*

However, I suggest by the tone of his letter and his home address I suspect the above was an observation as opposed to actually 'labouring in all weathers' himself.

We have already read above Adrian Gregory's three reasons for 'volunteering', the historian Niall Fergusson in his book *'The Pity of War'* (Penguin 1999) places exposure to the military the first out of the five suggestions he puts forward as to the reasons men join up. The others were: Female pressure, though as Alex Potter in his book *'Torquay and the Great War'* (Pen and Sword 2015) points out that a billboard encouraging women to 'shame' their men was met with such criticism that it was removed. This is followed by 'Peer Pressure' though this only seems to work where there are very high numbers in a given workforce, hence the 'Pals' battalions seen in the north of the country. Then 'Economic' and lastly 'Impulse', this may apply to men who were bored by their workplace and or having dreams of heroic deeds to be done, but for those who 'laboured in the already dangerous mines or quarries, this probably did not apply.

In the four months since the start of the war recruiting in the Penzance area appeared to follow the county's trend. Interestingly it also shows show that those who did volunteer wanted to join a local unit, the Territorials, as we have noted the servicemen in which, at this time, could still opt for Home Service only.

The Cornishman - Thursday 26 November 1914
PENZANCE NATIONAL RESERVE DISTRICT RECRUITING AREA 'Total, to date: Regulars 63, National Reserve 95, Territorials 150, Yeomanry 47, total 355 These figures include 16 men from the Isles of Scilly

That week:

Return of recruits for week ending November 21st, 1914: Regulars 2, from National Reserve 2, Territorials 12, Yeomanry, nil; total, 16.

However, a few did join a 'Pals' battalion, see below the West Briton and Cornwall Advertiser - Thursday 11 March 1915

By mid-November a clearer picture was emerging as Southern Command estimated that Devon had contributed 4,414 men to kitcheners New Army, but this represented just 0.62 per cent of the population, way below Birmingham's 3.35 and Warwick's 4.07 and even lower than Dorset's 1.44 and Somerset's 0.82, although higher than Worcester with 0.51 and Cornwall's startlingly low number of 0.28 per cent.

There were great differences in recruiting in other areas of the country:

Exeter and Plymouth Gazette - Friday 27th November 1914
But the numbers were not sufficient, and did not compare at all well with what had been done by some other counties. The percentage population worked out at about decimal 6, whereas in Gloucestershire it was more than double; Birmingham, five times; Warwickshire, six times- two millions of men already under arms meant about 4 per cent, of the population.

On the 16th December the German fleet bombarded Scarborough, Whitby and Hartlepool on the east coast. However, instead of being incensed or worried by this event the paper chose to publish a report that celebrated German seamanship:

Western Evening Herald - Thursday 17 December 1914
COOLNESS OP THE ENEMY. The Press Association correspondent says: According to as eye witness the bombardment of Scarborough was marked by extraordinary daring. "The German warships," he said "stole into the bay at about a quarter to eight this morning. There was nothing to indicate that they were not British. They manoeuvred into position, causing nearer to the pier than any battleship has ever done within living memory. One of

the oldest fishermen in Scarborough said no pilot could ever have dared to bring a warship as near inland as the German seaman did this morning.

However in the north east the reports were different:

Shields Daily News - Thursday 17 December 1914
CASUALTIES IN THE BOMBARDMENT. An official statement, issued by the Admiralty last night, estimated that at Hartlepool there were 29 killed and wounded; the casualties Scarborough were put 13, and Whitby two killed and two injured. This is not altogether in accordance with the figures given by Hartlepool correspondent, though in the ease of Whitby the variation is slight. Scarborough special correspondent says the killed number 15, and there are a large number of injured, but most the cases are slight. At Hartlepool, according to special correspondent, the killed number 47, and the injured probably 100.

Later the actual figures were Scarborough recorded 19 dead, Whitby three but Hartlepool 112 the biggest shock being that they were all non-combatants and contained equal numbers of being men, women and children. Hartlepool received the worst casualties because it became the scene of the only action during WW1 where units of land based British forces engaged the Germans. These were namely the Heugh and Lighthouse Coastal Batteries that suffered the death of nine soldiers. Royal Navy ships at sea and in the harbour who also engaged the enemy suffered five sailors killed.

The event was seized upon by the British government's propaganda department using Scarborough's seaside resort popularity, a therefore a non-military 'innocent' location, to create a poster encouraging enlistment:

Was it successful?

Locally it doesn't appear so. A month later by the end of January 1915 the recruiting enthusiasm actually waned in some rural communities of Yorkshire and appears to have bypassed others altogether. The local 'Green Howards' regiment, after holding a two recruiting marches through the area in April and May of 1915 only produced firstly nine and then 114 men. But as the town was in the old North Riding of Yorkshire, including Wensleydale, Ryedale and the regiment's large home town of Richmond, one would assume this would have generated more enlistment. Ultimately the men were raised, but from the large conurbations of the north east. Subsequently and with a complete volte face about the subject, those responsible for raising the unit, The North Riding County Association, came down decisively in support of the case for conscription[28].

There wasn't a great response nationally either. Here in the West Country there was little effect for example the numbers enlisting in Exeter were considerably weaker than that earlier in the year. In the rest of Devon the issues remained largely parochial with the same class distinctions, as the press reported on the recurring topic of farmers' sons not offering themselves as recruits. But in addition there was again the mention of compulsory service.

Exeter and Plymouth Gazette - Friday 18 December 1914

Devon Farmers' Union, appealing to farmers' sons to respond to the call to arms defence their homes and country. Mr. T. Kingwell said that at the last, meeting of the Council Exeter proposed a resolution Advocating compulsory service during the war, but was freely criticised and found little support. He thought that if the Government brought in compulsory service they would use discretion, and take the young men who could easily spared— there were thousands whose work could done women. Exeter last week on appeal for recruits, eight came forward.

A day later one West Country newspaper made a direct request:

Western Daily Press - Saturday 19 December 1914

RECRUITING APPEAL. "AVENGE SCARBOROUGH." The Recruiting Department issued from their headquarters yesterday the following striking incentive to recruiting :—" Avenge Scarborough, 'up and at 'em now.' The wholesale murder of innocent women and children demands vengeance. Men of England, the innocent victims' of German brutality call upon you to them., Show the German barbarians that Britain's shores cannot bombarded with impunity. Duty calls you now. Go to-day to tlx- nearest recruiting depot and offer your services for your King, home, and country."

It doesn't seem to have had the result the authorities hoped for. Could 'fatherly understanding or more probably a financial incentive work?

Exeter and Plymouth Gazette - Wednesday 23 December 1914

Recruits are being obtained from Devon at rate of about 25- 30 a day, but evidently there are still young men who are hanging back. In all probability, they are just waiting until after Christmas, but it cannot be too insistently pointed out to them that the call urgent. Those who desire to enlist, but still want to spend Christmas with their friends, can, by special arrangement, already recorded the Gazette," meet, their personal wishes socially and, at the same time, prove their patriotism. The arrangement those who sign can have over and above draw their Army pay.

Though reports from the Western Front must have been terribly shocking to read this report, especially at this time of year:

The Cornishman - Thursday 24th December 1914

...bits of jagged broken iron, like I gave you from Paris, sticking into your pal's innards — splosh! whoop! scatter of blood and things! Hell! "All right," fellow says: "it's in me side, but doesn't hurt." Then you see streak of pain rip across your pal's face, and you hear the scream that makes you sick,...... Oh, yes, the top note in a bombardment is the cry and howl of the

wounded pals. Some howls won't leave you. Poor beggars with bayonet rip will yelp like a dog all night. Another smothers up and croons husha-bye-babies they don't cry. They grunt or scream. And the grunt the worst, for it turns your liver to ice."

There were signs of resistance to central government collating information on the numbers of men who were able to be recruited into the services:

St. Austell Star - Thursday 24<u>th</u> December 1914
We hear the Mid Cornwall Division Parliamentary Recruiting Committee are making good program with their recruiting lists for each parish in the division, and a report may be expected at the of the year or early in January.... Nor is it a matter of mere collection of data for considerable difficulty has been experienced in encoring from some quarters the desired information.

Although for many hundreds of men on both sides in Flanders experienced the so called Christmas Truce of 1914 that arose spontaneously between several British and German infantry battalions. But not it must be said, if those in the opposite trench were Prussians. This does paints a rosy picture. However, as the historian Denis Winter points out, although the British might respect their brave enemies, initially they were the wearier of the two as they did not fully trust them.

A new year saw a boost in recruiting from those who worked in the China clay areas of the county, much to the obvious pleasure of the paper...

Cornish Guardian - Friday 01 January 1915
CLAY WORKS RECRUITS FROM BLADES AND TREGONISSEY. They number 86, which is eight per cent of the total population. Seeing there is so much being said about the slackness of the clay district in recruiting, is only fair to say that if the country as a whole could show as high a percentage as this part of the clay district, there would be a bigger Army that is required.....

Whether these were in effect those to whom we could ascribe an 'Economic' reason, as there had been layoffs in the early months of the war, I cannot tell. But I suspect this was initially the case then followed by 'Peer Pressure'.

Exeter and Plymouth Gazette - Friday 01 January 1915
We are glad notice improvement in the recruiting returns in many districts since Christmas, this being especially noticeable at Birmingham, where men have come forward in considerable numbers join the ranks.....

However, the same newspaper reports of a local Barnstaple man who clearly did not want his sons to enlist and ended in court:

Sgt. Williman, of the Ist Devons, one of the local recruiting officers, spoke to calling the defendant, he having learnt that the latter had three sons who were eligible for the Army. Witness was told that the sons were not home, and asked the defendant if he had any objection to their enlisting. He replied: "Yes, I am a road contractor." Defendant admitted his sons were of such age to able to enlist without his knowledge, but said witness could not see them, and commenced to rave about the house, and to swear, telling the witness, with an oath, that he could go away.

This also shows that the army at least in this area of Devon were 'bringing personal influence to bear' already; this addition then adding

….and those so stony-hearted and unpatriotic who do not respond these callous people must not be surprised if, hereafter, they are looked down upon their fellow men and women. As I have already said, there are signs of improvement with the recruiting figures from the West. We hope they be more than realised.

Obviously the Parliamentary Division reports were intended to provide information to be used alongside the use of some sort of coercion:

West Briton and Cornwall Advertiser - Monday 4th January 1915

*Yet the recruits have not been forthcoming. And it is stated that of the men who have joined the Army in Cornwall since the outbreak of war, more than half the number are married. There are yet many thousands of young men available. Further meetings are to be held in the Parliamentary Divisions…. In addition, returns are being made giving the names and addresses of all men of military age who have not joined, **with the object of bringing personal influence to bear** in cases where circumstances point to the conclusion that the men ought to be in the Army.*

In Devon desperate times seems to have brought desperate measures as there was a report that recruiting in one section of society was going well:

Western Times - Monday 01 March 1915

TRAMPS AND THE WAR

Fewer 'Roadsters' in Okehampton District.

A further slump in tramps was reported at the meeting of Okehampton Board of Guardians on Saturday, when the return presented the Master the Workhouse stated that the number for the fortnight had only been as compared with 50 in the corresponding period last year. Eight per week was the lowest number for this period of the year in the Master's experience. The Chairman (Mr. A. Guy Whipham) said 'evidently recruiting was going well among the tramp class'.

Which, I suggest, indicates just how desperate things had become.

Men of the counties in a 'Pals' Battalion:

West Briton and Cornwall Advertiser - Thursday 11th March 1915
THE WEST-COUNTRY SPORTSMEN'S BATTALION. _ The West country Company of the 2nd Sportsmen's Battalion of the Royal Fusiliers, which Capt. A. E. Dunn (formerly M.P. for the Mining Division) so splendidly recruited, were inspected at the Castle Yard, Exeter, on Monday, by Col. Western. The Mayor (Mr. J. G. Owen), addressing the troops, said they were men of Devon and Cornwall—Cornwall, whose motto was One and All." and Devon, whose motto was "Semper Fidelis." He was sure that no matter in what tight corner they found themselves they would remember the mottoes of those two counties and that they would bear in mind not only their oath of allegiance, but also the honour of the dear West Country which they belonged. He was sure they would always uphold the honour of the flag, and in the name of the City of Exeter he wished them God-speed, great glory, and a safe return.

The British army on the Western Front had received reinforcements from units that had been serving abroad plus many battalions of the British Indian army and, because of the dire situation the BEF found itself, Territorial units were also in the front line. They were all to be in action at the Battle of Neuve Chapelle on the 10th to 13th March. Previously Sir John French and the French Commander in Chief General Joffre had met on the 27th December in Chantilly when the British commander assured his counterpart that as far as he was concerned the main battles of the war were to be fought in Belgium and France. Joffre being told that Britain, first and foremost, would concentrate here and nowhere else. Although the politicians in London confirmed their General's statement a month later, they were in fact also looking at other places, so various plans were being discussed[29]. The French and British staff now discussed a small British offensive and the site chosen was this small village south of Armentieres, overlooked by the ridge named after the larger conurbation situated there, Aubers.

Western Times - Tuesday 16 March 1915
SIGNAL SUCCESS Of the British Offensive Movements AT NEUVE CHAPELLE "Eye Witness" Tells Story of Soldiers' Powers Press Bureau, Saturday Evening…. At 7.30 a.m. the 10th the battle began with a bombardment of a large number of guns and howitzers. Our men in the trenches describe this fire as being the most tremendous, both in point of noise and in actual effect, they have ever seen or heard The shrieking of the shells in the air, their explosions, and the continuous thunder the batteries all merged into one great volume sound. The discharges of the guns were so rapid that they sounded like the fire of a gigantic machine gun. During the thirty-five minutes continued our men could themselves freely, and even walk about perfect safety. Then the signal for the attack was given, and in less than half an hour almost the whole of the elaborate series of German trenches in and about Neuve Chapelle were in our hands. Except at one point there was hardly any resistance, for the trenches,

which in places were literally blotted out, were filled with dead and dying partially buried in earth and debris, and the majority of the survivors were in no mood for further fighting. To the north-east of the village, however, a body of Germans ensconced in some enclosures, still continued to hold out for a few hours. Our men then carried out three attacks but spite of the extreme gallantry with which they were conducted, failed to dislodge them; at about noon the arrival of reinforcements drove the Germans from their last stronghold in the village.......

British Soldiers' Dash Our success does not lie the fact that we have gained an extent of ground probably greater than has ever been gained in the space of so short a time since the commencement of the present form of trench warfare, that our men, in spite of the disheartening effects of months of inactivity in the trenches, have shown the utmost dash throughout these operations....

The above report from the Western Times is the only one I could find from a West Country newspaper, surprising as we know this was the first major offensive undertaken by the army. The one SW unit involved were the 2nd Devons within 23rd Brigade alongside units all returned from overseas in the newly created 8th Infantry Division. The attack was a successful one with most of the targeted areas captured within the first hours; however as with all battles on the Western Front there was a 'break in' but no 'break out'. Ultimately the Germans were able to bring in reinforcements and to hold the line, but it was farther back from the original.

I did notice in the report that nothing was mentioned about the efforts of the British Indian units of the 3rd and 7th Divisions who played a great part in the battles limited by successful outcome and whose magnificent memorial stands outside of the village to this day. However on the 18th March the St Austell star featured an interview with a local man who had been wounded at Ypres while serving with the Army Service Corps and states that the Ghurkahs were *'splendid and absolutely fearless'* adding that *'the Germans were absolutely afraid of them'*.

And in Cornwall attempts to increase recruiting continued:

The Cornishman - Thursday 1st April 1915
WEST YORKS REGIMENT. ROUT MARCH FROM PENZANCE TO ST. IVES..... Col. Warwick thanked the Mayor for his hearty and generous reception accorded them and he hoped that the percentage of recruiting in Cornwall would soon be raised from five to fifteen per cent....In response to the appeal at St. Ives one recruit was forthcoming.

The figures for No. 8 District for Friday totalled 71, which shows that recruiting is not being accelerated. Hampshire 31, Somerset 14, Devon 9, Cornwall 9, Wiltshire 6, Dorset 2. Total 71.

The soldiers of the Raj were in the minds of a few Christians who recognised the need for warm clothing:

<u>West Briton and Cornwall Advertiser</u> - <u>Saturday 3rd April 1915</u>

Helston Branch Queen Marys Needlework Guild have just sent the fourth bale of goods for the soldiers at the Front. The parcel contained four body belts, sixty pairs of socks, 23 shirts, 39 mufflers, one cap, one helmet, 45 pairs mittens and eight pairs of cuffs. A special parcel for the Indian soldiers contained six shirts, six vests, six chest protectors, and three pairs of mittens.

Neuve Chapelle had upset the German plans for their offensive but five weeks later The Second Battle of Ypres began. It was fought from 22 April – 25 May 1915 and is notorious in military history as it was the first mass use by Germany of poison gas on the Western Front. By the end of the battle British forces had withdrawn to a new line 3 miles closer to Ypres, thereby resulting in a compression of the salient. They again suffered horrendously with another 59,000 casualties. Meanwhile the Germans, suspicious that the British were using the spires of the Cloth Hall for artillery observation, shelled the building and its city with 17" Howitzers causing massive death and destruction. Sometime after the war's end they piously claimed that *"…the blame must not be laid on us for the gradual destruction of the magnificent buildings…"*. We should remember the same sentiments were expressed by the Allies after their destruction of the Abby of Monte Cassino in 1944.

The below appeared in *The Cornishman* newspaper on the same day that the second battle commenced. It mentions a lack of artillery 'shells', the first reference to the so called 'Shell Scandal' that would be the excuse to soon replace him with Douglas Haig.

SIR JOHN FRENCH.

It is not too much to add that Sir French is idolized by British in Flanders as is General Joffre the men the long, long line that starts from Switzerland. Nor it a misuse words to state that in the opinion of his German enemies, and our French and Belgian allies, Sir John French's tactics in the great battle of Ypres, place him in the ranks of the greatest commanders. When he gets his shells we shall hear more from him and his splendid and enthusiastic Army. Sir John is a little more grey than he was before the war. But the man is the picture of health, and how much to-day the world's future depends upon the health of Joseph Joffre and the French! The great commander of army the flower the aloe, which blooms only once in a century. It has not been necessary for us to reveal a commander since the Great Duke, for we now know that the early Afghan campaigns, the Crimea, the Boer War, and the frontier scraps were mere incident by comparison with the battles of the Aisne and that Battle of Ypres which the French call the Battle of Flanders. We now realize that Waterloo had only 24,000 British troops engaged, whereas Sir John has the present moment (may I say it) more than twenty times that at his disposal.

St. Austell Star - Thursday 8ᵗʰ April 1915

WOMEN AND WAR WORK. TO BE PAID AT SAME RATES AS MEN. Mr. Lloyd George has sent the following reply to Miss Sylvia Pankhurst, asked whether the Treasury agreement between the Board of Trade and Labour representatives would secure that women should receive equal pay for equal work with the men whom they might replace:— Dear Miss Pankhurst,—The words which you quote some would guarantee that women undertaking the work of men would get the tame piece-rates as men were receiving before the date of this agreement. That, of course, means that if the women turn out same quantity of work as men employed on the same job they will receive exactly the same pay.

Disturbing to some as this was it was considered as insignificant to the news of a week later. This provoked outrage and worldwide condemnation (for those neutral or supporting the Entente) when Sir John's report of the 23ʳᵈ appeared. It stated that the Germans had used gas on the Western Front:

The Cornishman - Thursday 29ᵗʰ April 1915

GERMANS USE POISONOUS GAS. PRESS BUREAU. Friday, 11.15 p.m.: Sir French communicates the following under date April 23ʳᵈ: Yesterday evening the enemy developed an attack upon the French to our left in the neighbourhood and Langemarck, the north of the Ypres salient. This attack was preceded by a heavy bombardment, the enemy at the same time making use of a large number of appliances for the production of asphyxiating gas.

The line shrank back towards the city of Ypres but did not break with the Belgians, French, British, Canadian, Australian and New Zealand units being rotated through the salient as they became available. Meanwhile although training of the New Armies continued the British Government became ever more concerned about the lack of voluntary recruitment.

For example there were many cases in Devon when recruiting parties were not made welcome and some even faced verbal hostility; *'A Huntsham farmer told soldiers'* they were not welcome on his property and a soldier retorted *"Why should we fight for you slackers?"* Unabashed the farmer asserted that he should be *'back in the trenches'*, not *'mucking about here*, adding *'I don't care a ____ if the Germans do come'* At Bradninch a man called out *'Us'll go when the* (sic) *varmer's sons go'*[30]

It would seem, logically, that the more the papers reported the appalling casualties and printed soldiers' letters from the front this would have the effect of deterring not encouraging recruitment. Also, initial female encouragement to shame their relations into going could now be more inclined to keep them safe at home.

Even so as the secondary partner to the French on the Western Front the British were obliged to once again keep on the offensive. After their loss of territory during the Battle of Neuve Chapelle the Germans had reinforced their units in the area especially on the rising ground immediately behind the now captured village, the previously mentioned Aubers

Ridge. The attack was not successful as the German defences had proved too strong. The covering fire for support of the attacking troops was not good enough as the resources were not available, it did not help that Kitchener sent over 22,000 shells from France to the Dardanelles a campaign ill conceived and would lead to the great betrayal of the West Country[31], [see below].

The intelligent use of women in the workforce was in part brought about by recruiting. Less than one year from the declaration of war the report in the St. Austell Star of Thursday 8th April 1915 above, had produced headlines and a story that illustrates a very real conundrum: Economy v Recruiting. This was followed by:

West Briton and Cornwall Advertiser - Thursday 13th May 1915
CORNISH WOMEN AND WORK.

Sir. L. C. Foster presided at a meeting of Liskeard and District Education Committee Monday, when the circular from the county re agricultural labour for women was considered. It suggested that District Committees in formulating their schemes might include the instruction of women in agricultural pursuits.—Canon Purcell: In the North of England they are doing it very largely.—The Chairman : But in the North England women are more accustomed to work than in Cornwall. —Canon Purcell: Don't you think it time they learnt:'—The Chairman : No doubt the committees of the four agricultural demonstrations to be held in the district will see if anything can be done.

Obviously the Home and Western Fronts were being integrated by the greater utilization of a previously unrecognised workforce. I have not been able to find a newspaper from the area that records anything about the Battle of Aubers, possibly because local battalions were not involved so I include one, with a large amount of 'spin', from London:

Evening Mail - Monday 17th May 1915
THE ATTACK ON AUBERS RIDGE. Below Armentires (sic) our line runs through the Bois Grenier, south-east of Laventie to Neuve Chapelle, Givenchy, and Cuinchy, on the western outskirts of La Basee. This has been the black spot of the week. Here it was that we stormed the slopes of the Aubers ridge, stormed them unsuccessfully and at heavy cost because we had not sufficient high explosives at our command to destroy the strong German entrenchments on the hilltops. But our men who fell on the Aubers slopes did not fall altogether in vain. The menace of the Aubers ridge deceived the enemy to withdraw his troops from regions further south to defend his salient at La Bassee. Though the attack failed we menace La Bassee still and hold in our front a large force of the enemy. Thus we are rendering service to the French in the Lens-Arras sector. And so from the sea to La Basses the fair land of Belgian and French Flanders is belted by the united armies of Belgium, France, and Britain. At no point has the enemy a favourable prospect of breaking through.

As we have read the attacks asked of the British by the French had very little gains. Even the French themselves, whose valiant 'Poilu' [Line infantry] attacked with the expected *'elan'* only to die in great numbers before German barbed wire, machine guns and the largest killer of all, the artillery. It is no wonder that Professor Spencer Jones titles his book concerning 1915 'Courage without Glory'

On the Home Front in the West Country, Devon led the way with the employment of women within the workforce:

The Western Times - Friday 2ⁿᵈ July 1915

The Emergency Committee the Torquay Chamber of Commerce is meeting to-day and the question of the readjustment of labour will be one that will receive attention. Such register, it thought, will enable the nation's power to utilised the greatest advantage. Paignton is already usefully employing women upon work formerly undertaken by men and the willingness women to help will probably result many more men being released for the services.

The lack of trained staff for vital war work lost to enlistment began to be a problem:

The Cornishman - Thursday 12ᵗʰ August 1915

Major Pike insists that there are 30,000 eligibles (sic) in Cornwall who ought to enlist, and points out that owing to the heavy casualties' in the DCLI the recruits from Cornwall are not enough to repair wastages. Mr. J. H. Collins is the latest, but not the only complainant that Cornish mining are suffering from the recruiting which has withdrawn considerable proportion of active young miners and middle aged men both from underground and service operations…… because wolfram is vital to the manufacture of steel.

Throughout the war a balance tried to be maintained between those wanted by the services, mainly the army but as the war widened the Royal Navy and industry. Who were going to make the rifles, the artillery shells even the uniforms and badges of the men being pleaded with to join up ? The situation was dire at the start of the war for example Territorial units had to give up their modern Lee Enfield rifles much needed by those proceeding to the front, the weapons being replaced, admittedly, just while undergoing training with old Japanese Askari rifles.

Sir John French lost his position as Commander in Chief of the Western Front later in the year over the previously referred to 'Shell Scandal'. In his defence the control of such matters was limited, being in the hands of politicians and industrialists who had turned to recruitment of a different kind, women. They would now be encouraged to do their bit and work in the factories, on the buses and waterways even in the shipyards much to the consternation of the men and with some protest from their unions.

Each new battalion needed a minimum number of men and volunteering had increased the numbers for one unit to that required. On the 25ᵗʰ August 1915 the 10ᵗʰ (Service) Battalion DCLI, raised by the personal intervention of Quiller-Couch and the Mayor of Truro, was finally 'adopted' by the War Office. These men were destined to be a Pioneer unit providing vital building and construction support on the Western Front from May 1916 until the end of the war.

Given the diminishing numbers of qualified men in the mines many within the industry would have been hoping for the return of many who had volunteered, but this was not to be for 221 new recruits. On the 28th September 1915 these men from the mining districts of Cornwall, who had originally volunteered for the DCLI, were transferred, joining the newly created specialist 251 Tunnelling Company at Hayle, Cornwall. In his book *Battle Beneath the Trenches* written about the unit, author Robert Johns reports with some amusement that in such companies, comprising as they were very well qualified miners from the world over, discipline was lax. *The word 'sir' was more likely to be 'mate' or in the case of 251, 'Cap'n' or 'me ansome', saluting at best would have been sketchy and at worst totally forgotten.* The home of these Cornishmen on the Western Front was Bethune and their work-place, the infamous tunnels at Givenchy and Cambrin. The book lists a total of 21 such companies including two Canadian that contained Cornish miners, one of these volunteers, born in Liskeard, Cornwall, had been living in Los Angeles with his wife but joined the 'colours' in September 1917. It is very sad to say that Sapper Frank Reynolds was killed in action just three days before the Armistice.

Another Cornishman, John French, a tin miner born at Redruth in 1892 also served on the Western Front in the 254th Tunnelling Company. In 1917 at Passchendaele near Ypres he received a battlefield commission and the award of the Military Cross for 'conspicuous bravery'. Although he lived to see the Armistice he died age 37 in the United States, like Frank Reynolds, he was another one of the thousands from the poorer West Country who had gone to seek their fortune[32].

Mining is an inherently dangerous occupation. Those on the Western Front had to contend not only with the inherent dangers but also that fighting underground also took place against German miners. Consequently, these very brave men were at large treated with great respect by those who served on the surface above them.

In Britain those who were engaged in essential work were first issued with an arm band followed by a lapel badge. Unfortunately this was abused that seems to have been a nationwide problem as some of those wishing to avoid being questioned about enlistment or registation under the Derby Scheme had resorted to creativity.

Cornish Guardian - Friday 20 August 1915

Mr. Lloyd George has determined to stop the scandal of the bogus war service badge. Rules have been issued by him under Section R of the Munitions of War Act, one of which reads:—
No person shall, except with the authority of the Minister, make, sell, issue, or wear any badge supplied or authorised by the Minister, or any colourable imitation thereof, or any badge or other distinctive mark calculated or intended to suggest that wearer thereof is engaged on munitions work or other work for war purposes.

Munitions Essential Workers badge, appropriately based on the
Royal Artillery uniform button of the mid Victorian period.

To the authorities there was apparently still resistance in Cornwall to volunteering. As a consequence appeals also voiced the fact that unless more men could be found conscription could become a reality:

The West Briton and Cornwall Advertiser - Monday 11 October 1915
RECRUITS PROM PENRYN AND FALMOUTH. SIXTEEN OBTAINED IN SATURDAY'S RALLY. Sixteen names were handed in as the result of a recruiting rally at Penryn and Falmouth on Saturday. Major C. S. Goldman, M.P., and officers and men of Cornwall R.G.A. took part in the rally …….Major Goldman said was addressing himself particularly to those, who perhaps for very good reasons, said the call had not come to them. The call now was far more imperative than it had been. Take, for instance, the last battle. The French soldiers were able to pierce and penetrate the whole line of the enemy. Ours had only been able to partially penetrate, largely due to insufficiency of numbers. They wanted to weld the manhood of the nation in collective effort to overwhelm their enemies. His colonel had succeeded in securing few vacancies in the Cornwall R.G.A., and was an eminently favourable opportunity for men of Penryn to join that corps, because they would be doing their duty at Pendennis Castle, yet still be among their families and friends. He advised and implored them to join at once and not let the opportunity slip. Men hated and loathed the word conscription, but those men still hanging back were producing that system. Col. Gray (Penryn) also made appeal, and Capt. the Rev. P. Bacon (chaplain) said every county except Cornwall had a Territorial Battalion at the front, and the 5th D.C.L.I. had not gone because they had <u>not enough men</u>.

The battle the Major had referred to had been fought in around and within the French mining town of Loos. Between the 25th until the 8th October 1915 the British, in a combined operation with the French in a separate sector of the front, had been able to break in but not through the German lines. There was great bravery but terrible loss of life; and the gas attack referred to below had been made by the British, but with poor results. There was no wind on the day so this ghastly 'war winning weapon' affected the British forces more than their enemies.

St. Austell Star - Thursday 25th November 1915
One of the finest of the gallant deeds recorded was that of Piper Laidlaw, of the Kings Own Scottish Borderers, who, piping his company somewhat shaken from the effects of gas, mounted the parapet, marched up and down, and played his company out of their trench and on to the assault, only desisting when he fell wounded.

The so called 'learning curve' of the British army, a term beloved by many revisionist historians, still had a very long way to go. And as we have seen, so had recruiting. However, in Devon one town did send many of its sons off to fight.

Illfracombe, on the north Devon coast had the reputation, during the Victorian and Edwardian period, as an up-market seaside resort with many thousands of tourists arriving by a direct rail service from London. This town provided around 500 men for the conflict encouraged by a scheme where their photographs were placed for the public to see and therefore admire, in a local photographer's shop window, 'Peer' pressure obviously working in this case. The originators of this scheme were a local headmaster, Mr. Lord and the Chairman of the local council Mr. Andrews. How are we today to view such a patriotic impulse as the memorial records the deaths of 99 or around 20 percent, one in five who served.

Devon's War Memorial, Exeter

How could we end the war, how were we to encourage our ally Russia that had suffered appalling casualties far greater than our own, not to make a separate peace with the Central Powers? How were we to answer the appeal on the 2nd of January 1915 from their Grand Duke Nicholas for a diversionary attack on the Turks[33] by Britain and France after Russian set backs on the Armenian/Georgian front? Putting promises to France aside the answer, provided for H. H. Asquith the British Prime Minister and his War Council, came from Winston Churchill, First Lord of the Admiralty. It could be found at the far end of the Mediterranean and not France or Belgium. The Dardanelles promontory juts into the sea, protecting the channel that also bears its name, famed in antiquity as the 'Hellespont' leading to The Sea of Marmara. It led then to Istanbul, ancient Constantinople, the then capital of The Ottoman Empire and a member of the Central Powers.

Capture or threaten their capital Churchill declared and the Ottomans would withdraw from the war thus allowing direct contact with Russia via the Bosporus and the Black Sea. He had to convince the war cabinet and finally did so after receiving the grudging support of the Secretary of State for War, Field Marshall Lord Kitchener.

CHAPTER SIX

The Great Betrayal: Dardanelles and Suvla Bay

As Peter Hart succinctly puts it: *'one thing is certain: Germany would never be beaten by an ill conceived adventure launched against Turkey. There was no back door to Germany, no easy route to victory; no allies propping her up, the removal of which could cause collapse'*. He goes on to show that even apart from the above, geographically, any attempt to move armies through the Balkan mountain ranges would meet with defeat. However, why did it appeal, why did the War Council, who must accept joint responsibility for the venture as they approved Churchill's idea, was made up not only of politicians but also their senior military advisers? Especially when all would have been aware of Britain's own doctrine as stated in the War Office's Manuel of Combined Operations that 'enough has been said ...to demonstrate the *impracticability of landing troops now-a-days in the face of opposition'* formulated as early as 1905 after a staged seaborne 'invasion' of Clacton resulted in the acknowledgement that *'modern weapons had greatly added to the difficulties of a force attempting an opposed landing'*[1].

Briefly, Turkey had been growing weaker militarily during the last century and had been propped up by Britain in the main plus France. This old empire was seen as a bulwark against Russia gaining what they now promised to supply, a short ice-free route to the Mediterranean and the city of Istanbul/Constantinople. The so-called 'sick man of Europe had recently been deprived of most of her Balkan empire, including Bulgaria, Romania and Greece. Her once domination of the area, stretching nearly to Vienna, now amounted to a large 'toe hold' on the edge of Europe.

The campaign is recognised as a poorly led operation. But if it had been successful and Turkey had been removed as an ally of Germany and Austria-Hungary, then the soldiers of the Entente powers, including many hundreds from the West Country would have been spared the Mesopotamian [Iraq] and Palestine campaigns (see below).

Historically, the man chosen to lead the military action, initially just to support the Royal Navy with the idea that they probably would not be called upon, was General Sir Ian

Hamilton. He was the 'wonder' of his age, highly experienced, personally brave, thoughtful and the most senior general in the army, unfortunately, to quote from the recent TV series: *Doing something great is overrated, people expect it of you all the time'*. However, the Devons' had little to thank him for as he had ordered the attack on Wagon Hill on the 6th January 1900 during the battle of that name outside of Ladysmith. It was here that three companies of their 1st Battalion suffered 28 percent loses with every officer either killed or wounded except the Colonel. See above the Totnes Weekly Times Saturday 20th October 1900.

His career, when put against others of a similar age had produced a man of wide experience and undoubted personal bravery as he had famously been recommended twice for a VC, neither of which he received. This was not because this was undeserved but, in the first instance, because it thought that as a young officer other opportunities were sure to arrive. The second because he was now considered too old and that such awards should go to younger officers, though after the first recommendation he did attend Queen Victoria to describe the action. But he then missed out on a staff college place as he was requested by Lord Roberts as his military secretary [a.d.c.] in India. Would the staff college course have helped him at the Dardanelles, we will of course never know, but many who passed [psc] were frankly not brilliant in their senior roles either.

Later, while purportedly returning to England on leave, he arranged an attachment to the Gordon Highlanders and took part in the Sudan Campaign. Back in India he reformed the musketry school of the Indian Army and saw active service in Burma plus taking on the role of the Quartermaster General. His success in these rolls and personal bravery lined him up for service in South Africa where he again garnered laurels in command and the praise of those serving under him, including Horace Smith-Dorian. Later as an observer of the Russo-Japanese War he wrote an excellently received book. This concerned the conflict and controversially he then wrote papers pointing out the outdated training and tactics of the British Army when faced with modern weapons and smokeless powder. Even the German General Staff Journal, the '*Militär Wochenblatt*' praised him as being probably the most experienced soldier in any army in the world, high praise indeed and he was obviously considered the man who would succeed, come what may[2].

But, in the Gallipoli Association Journal of Spring 2015 the writer John Lee stated that in the lead up to the campaign '*Hamilton was dispatched with incredible speed, with an inadequate staff thrown together in a couple of days (and denied his friend Ellison as chief of staff in favour of Kitchener's choice, Walter Braithwaite). He was given little or no information about his troops or the enemies troops, was warned that 29th Division was only 'on loan' to him and might be recalled at any time, was denied any access to the staff studies of the Dardanelles region (including the 1906 report that it should never be attacked with less than 150,000 troops – preferably Greek!) and was flatly denied the reasonable request for some aircraft to assist the operation. The whole affair was to be done 'on the cheap' at a time when Great Britain really could not afford to mount a second major operation of war.*

The event as a whole was over optimistic, mismanaged, misjudged and led to 'mission creep' on a grand, tragic scale that ultimately led to withdrawal leaving the straits to a successful blockade.

The only part of the campaign I wish to look at in any detail are the landings at Suvla Bay on the 9th of October 1915 and the 2nd South Western Mounted Brigade and its two Devon Yeomanry units. These were the only men of Devon and Cornwall who were to serve in this disastrous campaign – apart from a number, obviously, who would have been members of other army battalions[3]. Initially they were attached to the 11th (Northern) Division, under the command of Major General Hammersley – see below.

These men had volunteered to join their local yeomanry units and comprised mostly Devonians and one squadron of Cornishmen. They had done so, obviously, in the anticipation of riding to battle. I suspect many of their ranks contained young men whose notions of warfare consisted of bugles, sabres and thankful pretty women hanging on their every word when they returned as heroes. What they got were butchers and bunglers, heat, flies and no horses. The whole of their Brigade were now dismounted as of September 1915, just one month earlier and at Suvla were tasked with digging trenches.

Lions and Donkeys?

At Suvla there was muddle, there was indecision and terrible leadership of troops who had undergone basic training at the most. These men deserved far better than these foisted on Hamilton, so called 'dug outs'. Unfortunately the British army still used the outdated practice of seniority and not health or more importantly, military competence. These were:

Major General The Honourable J. Lindley. 55 years of age, brought from retirement to command the 53rd (Welsh) Division; resigned his command at the Battle of Suvla telling Hamilton that he felt he had lost all control.

Brigadier General Sir William Sitwell, age 55. His previous career promised an officer of great ability, not so as his dismal performance at Suvla was so bad that he was sacked by Major General Sir Philip Hammersley age 57, himself in a state of nervous exhaustion, having completely lost control of his brigade. In fact Hammersley had suffered a complete nervous collapse at the start of the war, requiring hospitalization, but had been brought from retirement to command the 11th Division. He failed conspicuously to exercise any form of control, again at Suvla, suffering a nervous collapse and was invalided home.

One pick from someone who had experience of the Western Front was General Sir Walter Braithwaite 50, Hamilton's Chief of Staff. He tried to emulate the command style of Helmuth von Moltke with his 'mission led' command style, where you allow the man on the spot to decide on his own plans. Unfortunately, those under his command were more used to the top down approach. They were obviously unfit or too set in their ways, too inexperienced and responded poorly with a consequent lack of coordination. Those officers who were sent home were awarded medals even though it can be considered that they had been put into positions of authority way beyond their competence. Overall it appears that the army betrayed the very men it commanded.

The 2nd had immediately to deal with the ghastly site of unburied dead men, mules and horses with the accompanying smell in the high heat and the attention of the million of flies attracted to the corpses. Unlike what we think of as the sunny Mediterranean the weather turned dramatically from the previous searing heat to heavy rain, sleet and by November, snow. The rain became so bad that men were actually drowned as storms brought volumes of water cascading down the gullies and hills of Suvla Bay. They were 'lucky' in that they 'only' lost 11 men killed in action, plus 13 later through wounds or illness after they were withdrawn in the December and three more that had been sent home because of ill health. For men who must have considered themselves 'somebody' within their small communities this must have been a bitter pill to swallow. Hamilton was decidedly unimpressed with his generals but also seemed to lack confidence in his own decision making, instead, contacting Kitchener who replied *'If you deem it necessary to replace Stopford, Mahon and Hammersley, have you any competent generals to take their place. From your report I think Stopford should be sent home. This is a young man's war, and we must have commanding officers that will take full advantage of opportunities which occur but seldom. If, therefore, if any generals fail, do not hesitate to act promptly. Any generals I have available I will send you*[4]. Hamilton as the senior officer is ultimately to blame for such issues and should have insisted on his own ideas being paramount. They were not, he was recalled on the 14th October and never held a combat command again; on the same day the Cornishman carried a report that is beyond tragedy:

Cornishman - Thursday 14th October 1915
PROGRESS IN GALLIPOLI. 300 YARDS GAINED. PRESS BUREAU, Thursday.
Sir Ian Hamilton reports that during the past month the fighting Suvla Bay has not been a scale calling for special reports. Every night there have been patrol action, bomb attacks and the rushing of houses, and as result have gained during this period an average little over 300 yards along the whole centre —four miles of the Suvla front.

Averaging out to about 30 feet per day.

A week later:

Cornishman - Thursday 21st October 1915

LOSSES GALLIPOLI. In answer to question put him Bar. R. L. Outhwaite in the House Commons, Mr. H. J. Tennant gave the following particulars: of the casualties in the Dardanelles Expeditionary Force:

	Officers	Other Ranks
Killed or died of wounds	*1,185*	*17,772*
Wounded	*2,632*	*66,220*
Missing	*383*	*8,707*

The casualties the Australian and New Zealand Forces are as follow:

	Officers	*Other Ranks*
Killed or died of wounds	*335*	*5,664*
Wounded	*884*	*29,180*
Missing	*52*	*2,076*

The total casualties from all causes amount to 96,899

Exeter and Plymouth Gazette - Thursday 21 October 1915

Mr. Tennant informed Lieut- Commander Wedgwood that the officer who was in command of the troops that landed at Suvla Bay was longer in any command. He did not think it would be in the public interest to say I more on the subject at present.

Many were unprepared and only partially trained, their dead and wounded had answered Kitchener's and The Empire's call and by doing so put their faith in its generals. From the start to its sad ending the men performed near miracles alongside territorial volunteers and full time soldiers plus those from France and her colonies, Sikhs, Ghurkas and others from our Empire, plus Russian Jews and of course the magnificent Anzacs.

The overall problems with the campaign are well covered in several major works including one dedicated to the events in this area in particular: *'Suvla'* by Stephen Chambers, plus those on the campaign as a whole: *Gallipoli* by Peter Hart, Peter Liddle in *'Britain in the Widening War'*, Michael Forrest *'The Defence of the Dardanelles'* and an organisation devoted to its remembrance *'The Gallipoli Society'*. And finally, deservedly so, one dedicated to the brave Turkish soldiers who defended their country, Edward Erickson's *'Gallipoli. The Ottoman Campaign'*.

Western Times - Tuesday 21 December 1915

BRITISH TROOPS Moved from Suvla Bay and Anzac Cove Press Bureau, Monday. The War Office makes the following announcement: All the troops at Suvla and Anzac, together with their guns and stores, have been successfully transferred with insignificant casualties, to another sphere of operations.

The above was the only real success of the whole campaign. It was meticulously planned by Sir Charles Munro who replaced Hamilton and by the 9th of January 1916 all of the men had been evacuated, miraculously without any losses. The press report above is extremely disingenuous therefore in suggesting a 'transfer', as with Dunkirk it was defeat resulting in retreat.

However, north Devon had not emerged without casualties. This letter home from Sergeant Frank Cater although describing their experiences arrived after they had left the peninsula and returned to Egypt:

North Devon Herald –Thursday 13th January 1916

For about a week we were subjected to sundry shellings,(sic) but happily we did not suffer a single casualty. On the following Sunday, however, the Turks commenced to shell a couple of our guns which were in the vicinity. The shells were bursting all around us, and unfortunately one killed Major Greig, officer commanding C Squadron. The death of so popular an officer naturally cast a gloom over the regiment. On the following day I was of the party of five N.C.O.'s told off to go into the first line of trenches to see how things were worked there. It was quite an experience. There are miles and miles of trenches, and each one bears a familiar name. For instance, there is Piccadilly Circus, branching off into Bond-street; Dublin-street, etc.' and then there is an arch called the Marble Arch. It's really necessary to have names of some sort, otherwise it would be impossible to find one's way about. After remaining about a week in the dug-outs our squadron went into the trenches for twenty-four hours. We had a couple of trips, and then we were helping to man the trenches for eight days. I was put on outpost duty with six men, forming double sentries. . . . . With the break of day we returned to the fire trench; going on outpost duty again in the night. . . In the evening we had to go sand-bagging, building up the communicating trench, the bullets whizzing overhead the while, some of them hitting the bags, but fortunately missing us. The next night we had a much more risky job. The ——— Regiment on our right had pushed forward and established an advanced post, and it was up to us to do the same. I was told off with a party of eight. . . . and after cutting our own wire we advanced about 100 yards and started building what we call a grouse box. The remainder of the squad were engaged in passing out sandbags. We were extremely lucky in getting the wall high enough for shelter without drawing much fire from the Turkish trenches. We had to hold that box the following day and night, when another box was formed between ours and the ——— Regiment. There wasn't much risk of snipers, because there was no need for us to put our heads above the parapet, begin supplied as we were with periscopes. The next night a party of bomb throwers went out to cover a wiring party, and they were unfortunate in that they lost two men killed and one wounded. We also had three men wounded by a shell, and another man killed and two wounded in a 'grouse box.' I forgot to state that while in the dug-outs a shell landed here and killed Sergt. Symons (Swimbridge) and Corpl. Ackland, and wounded two others. . . We are on the move again this evening—going to Anzac, the right base of Chocolate Hill—the scene of the great fight during the first landing, when it was taken and re-taken three times. . . .

It is beyond the scope of this book but more trials were to come for the 2nd. They were now in Egypt and lost their yeomanry status much to their chagrin. Although other units who had been at Gallipoli were remounted, the two Devonshire Regiments were amalgamated on the 21st of December 1915 becoming infantry of the 16th (Devon Yeomanry) Battalion of the Devonshire regiment. They became part of the 74th (Yeomanry) Division of the Egyptian Expeditionary Force whose divisional insignia, a broken spur, represented their change of status. Their fiercest battle in Palestine was yet to come as on the 3rd December 1917 near Jerusalem, sadly, they suffered over 300 dead. Finally owing to the German so called 'Kaiserschlacht' attacks of March 1918 the 16th Devons then served on the Western Front up to the cessation of hostilities on the 11th November of that year. Finally the majority returned home in March 1919.

The first two years of the conflict had produced little good news and extremely high casualty rates that obviously must have contributed to the reluctance of many in the south west to serve King and Country.

But what of elsewhere and, were we a United Kingdom?

West Country Yeomanry at Gallipoli.

Royal 1ˢᵗ Devon Yeomanry	**Royal North Devon Yeomanry**
HQ Exeter	HQ Barnstaple
A Squadron Thorverton	A Squadron Holsworthy
B Ottery St Mary	B Barnstaple
C Totnes	C South Molton
D Bodmin (Cornwall)	D Great Torrington
West Somerset Yeomanry	*Brigade Troops*
HQ Taunton	Somerset Royal Horse Artillery, Taunton
A Squadron Wellington	Ammunition Column, Taunton
B Taunton	Army Service Corps, Weston-s-Mare
C Bridgewater	Field Ambulance RAMC Frome
D Yeovil	

CHAPTER SEVEN

A Kingdom United?

It would seem that enthusiasm or even excitement in the far south west about the war was apparently nowhere near that claimed or had been experienced in other parts of the UK.

However, on the British mainland I found that reports of recruiting, even in large conurbations, varied. This is also true as to the information to be gleaned from modern writers concerning the areas referred to. If we take Leeds for example Stephen Wade writes that Lord Kitchener wanted 100,000 men for his New Armies and that *'The response for the Pals' battalions was astonishing, throughout the war, Leeds was to have almost 90,000 men fighting in the services, and 9,460 were killed in action.* He strikes rather an optimistic note adding that *'As was the case throughout the land, men would sign up for a range of regiments, but the bulk of the volunteers joined up with the 'Pals' or the 'Bantams' battalions'*[1]. But the latter only after January 1915 when permission had been granted to call upon men of this stature.

If we contrast his statements with that of Edward Spiers who writes that *'Although the outbreak of war reportedly produced 'a ready response' in Leeds, the town had never had a strong military tradition, and it took until 16 August* (sic) *before the local Territorial battalions, the 6th and 7th West Yorkshires (Leeds Rifles) reached their full strength.* He admits that it took only four days to raise 1,275 men for a business 'Pals' battalion that excluded artisans and manual workers. However, this social exclusivity, and the failure to raise two workers' battalions, exacerbated class divisions in Leeds. He references a report in the Leeds Weekly Citizen of 2nd October 1914 with the headline: *'Why Recruiting Stopped'...There had been no public protest, no outspoken contempt, but just silence and a huge drop in the rate of recruiting'*[2].

Not all northern towns responded in the same exclusive way. It is of some interest that in Burnley, near the Lancashire mill town of Accrington, although a group calling itself the *Frontiersmen* originally intended to recruit exclusively from young business men, bank clerks and shop assistants, by implication 'white collar' workers. This excluded 'blue collar' manual workers, but because of a shortage the actual result reflected a more cross section of the town as a company of the Accrington 'Pals' battalion came from the latter. It has also been put forward that a slump in the cotton industry, besides 'manly patriotism', encouraged such recruiting[3].

In the Yorkshire countryside there seems to have been a varied response with some areas following a similar pattern to that in the West Country. This was reflected across much of Wensleydale and Ryedale producing all sorts of speculation as to the reason why there were few recruits, at meetings in Hawes and Pickering local recruiting officers found few men coming forward and even encountered jeers and heckling. At Hawes another attempt produced only one or two recruits while after the 3rd of October nobody at all. It was felt that in these isolated communities men felt little fear of invasion or the need to enlist. They seemed to regard war as something that soldiers did or saw no reason to volunteer as 'conscription was bound (*if needed*) to follow', besides, because of labour shortages they were receiving higher wages[4].

Bradford Weekly Telegraph - Friday 30 October 1914
Sir Arthur Goodwin said the Lord Mayor and himself were unfortunately beyond the recruiting age. but there were plenty of young men to take a share of service for our country.

Hull Daily Mail - Friday 01 January 1915
Lincoln, December 30th. Dear Sir, I was very pleased yesterday to receive the six good recruits you sent in from Brigg. I trust you may able send some more shortly. We want men very much for the county regiment.

Blackpool Gazette & Herald - Friday 01 January 1915
It was decided that the county agents should arrange meetings in the agricultural districts, with the object of enrolling recruits for different regiments from among the farmers' and their servants. The Blackpool Committee is to leave the holding of meetings outside of the borough in hands of the county but an active campaign is to be continued within the borough. As a result of the activities of the Committee two men Peter McDermott and Edward McDermott have been added to the roll of honour. They have joined the Scots Guards and left Blackpool on Wednesday.

What of the rural east of England:

Boston Guardian - Saturday 01 May 1915
ANOTHER RECRUIT.—Mr. A\. Hubbert, Station-road, platelayer on the G.N.R., has joined the Royal Engineers as sapper, and undergoing the necessary military training at Longmoor, Hants.

A month later The Lincolnshire Echo published a quote from the authoritative Manchester Guardian *'The attempt to stampede the country into conscription is now in full swing'* that seems to confirm that the number of volunteers required are not coming forward in such numbers to fill the depleted and rapidly depleting ranks.

As the nation had been told we were fighting for 'plucky little' Belgium, understandably the British attitude to those fit young refugees or Belgian residents in this country who did not volunteer could have caused great friction, hence:

Newmarket Journal - Saturday 05 June 1915
BELGIANS CALLED TO ARMS. M. Hyman the Belgian Minister in London ordering all Belgian of eighteen to twenty five years of age were to obtain from the police a form of enrolment before June the 20th and men arriving later to enrol themselves within 15 days of landing in England. The men so enrolled will be called upon to report themselves before a recruiting committee.

Farther south in the city of Oxford, a much smaller, and a more university dominated city with a 1901 census figure of under 50,000 as opposed to 162,100 today. Exhortations to enlist from the 'Gown' to 'Town' pointing out German atrocities against the working man were received with some disdain. A.L.Smith, the Master of Balliol College recorded that working men, those trying to better educate themselves by attending classes run by the Working Education Association, still held strong class prejudices. Evidently, in their opinion, recruiting drives did not have any effect as *'they wouldn't be any worse off under German rule'*[5].

Oxfordshire Weekly News - Wednesday 09 June 1915
A large crowd assembled, including many persona from the villages. The recruiting sergeants met with a fairly good response, but not what it should have been considering the number of men about. At eight o'clock an adjournment was made to the Corn Exchange where a set of military pictures was given, including parts of the Army Film. Sir Algernon Peyton, Bt. made a speech, in which he referred to the necessity for more men at the Front. Oxfordshire and the Bicester district had done well in recruiting, but there were thousands of young men about who had not offered their services…... the sergeant spoke an instance ware seven able-bodied men in one household but none of them had gone.

A month later the same paper that covered the rural villages in the north of Oxfordshire, reported that during that period of those volunteering 41percent, 14 out of 34 were rejected, such being the state of health in these communities.

Men had been rejected since the start of the conflict for not being fit or tall or just too infirm for one reason or another. It therefore seems a rather desperate idea to recruit servicemen who for want of height earned the sobriquet 'Bantam'. The Halesworth Times and East Suffolk Advertiser of Tuesday 05 October 1915 carried a plea for men who were from five feet to five feet two inches tall to apply for a new battalion of the Suffolk Regiment comprising others of the same stature and for service in various units including the Royal Artillery and Royal Flying Corps. This was not the first authorisation for those men of five feet to five feet three inches tall to enlist. They were not the first.

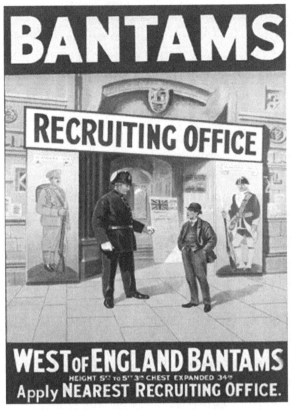

The Gloucester Regiment also raised a Bantam Battalion.

In Storey and Kay's *Northumberland and Tyneside's War'* they write that although these heavily populated areas had seen spectacular results with recruiting by late 1914 enthusiasm had diminished and consequently, on the 13th January 1915, a Durham Bantam Battalion was authorised by the War Office. Unfortunately this unit did not do well as physically as like many of the volunteers throughout the country although willing, they could not take the enormous strain of trench 'life' and were replaced by non-bantams. There were very few of the original volunteers remaining by 1918 in their original units or even the army. However, this was not always the case as Michael Taylor points out in his book *'No Bad Soldiers'* (Helion Press 2022) that offers a much more nuanced examination of the army's 119th 'Bantam' Brigade.

Halifax, in the (then) West Riding of Yorkshire had a chequered history when it comes to voluntary recruiting, David Millichope writes that *'...we could say that only half of Halifax's eligible men joined the armed forces with any degree of enthusiasm. The other half not only held back but took several positive steps to prevent it happening. Not only had they resisted the many campaigns to get them to enlist voluntarily, they had publicly refused to enlist when canvassed by the Derby scheme and then put considerable effort into gaining exemption through the military service tribunals'[6].*

In the West Country, Torquay in Devon as with much of the country volunteer enlistment had peaked in the week 5th to the 12th of August 1914 with just below 70 men volunteering. There was another high during the 2nd to the 9th and then fell to between 12 to 18 men per week until December 16th. Overall the return with a figure of 101 was higher than all four

West Country counties as a whole due to high unemployment within the service sector as a result of the reduction in tourism[7]. In comparison during the same period in the West Country this figure was 88 with only Southern Ireland in its agricultural districts being lower at 32.

However, across the country recruitment rates varied enormously. From August to the 4th November 1914 in Southern Scotland for example 288 men per 10,000 volunteered. Comparatively Dublin, Belfast, Wicklow and Kildare returned nearly four times this rate at 127, though appeals to both Nationalist and Unionist politics would have played a great part in this greater response. Around 75,000 residents of Ireland had enlisted by April 1915; however, some 40 percent came from just the six largely Protestant counties in the north[8]. The number for Southern Scotland shows the greater geographical recruitment area included the Highlands and outer islands[9]. Also unlike the previously mentioned lack of a military tradition in the Leeds area I would propose that, especially the Highlands of Scotland, there was a strong tradition of enlistment in the armed services. This also could have been boosted because prices had risen and as the Aberdeen Evening Express reported on the 4th August that because of the outbreak of hostilities *'Fifteen thousand workers in the fish and allied trade, with their thousands of dependants have had their means of support withdrawn'*.

As we have seen above the pattern of a rush to enlist in the south west was followed by a striking reduction in overall numbers. Looking at Bristol for example on the 24th November it was reported in the local press that only one recruit enrolled[10].

Conscription was inevitable as the last vestige of voluntary enlistment, the Derby Scheme, was not a success and even though the national government was predominately Liberal it was left with no further option[11.] By the scheme's closing date 38 percent of single men and 54 percent of married men had still failed to enlist and, as we have seen in Halifax, many had refused on their doorstep. Also throughout the British Isles, with fake exempted service badges, some men had even attempted to avoid registration.

Conclusion

Insufficient numbers of volunteers throughout the British Isles failed to enlist for three main reasons: Firstly, something that certainly was not just restricted to the two counties is the lack of a feeling of a status within society. We see a distinction between the 'blue collar' and those such as the Penzance solicitors, the residents of affluent Bristol's elevated suburbs such as Clifton and Redland, the Leeds *Frontiersmen* and even the pre-war Territorials and Yeomanry, just had the Victorian Rifle Volunteers, men who identified with the status quo. They believed that they had a place in a stratified, extremely class conscious society as opposed to for example Cornish china clay, Devon and Oxfordshire agricultural workers or many Yorkshiremen who did not. A proportion of these latter men took the 'King's Shilling' primarily when forced or because of unemployment and subsequent increased poverty. The reasons for this include inflation that now began a precipitous rise and the price of basic foodstuffs caused initially by those who were able to hoard.

Secondly the poor health of many in the largest class of the country, the poorer people who relied on the capriciousness of the market and in many cases the generosity of their employer. As we have seen many were treated as mere chattel to be used or discarded without a thought as what problems this would bring to their previous employees.

Thirdly, although it is self evident that war is a dangerous business, a statement so obvious that it needs some explanation as to why I would write it. Although not part of the British Expeditionary Force immediately sent to the continent in August 1914 the 1st Battalion the Devonshire Regiment joined the 14th Brigade, 5th Division, alongside the 1st DCLI and came under artillery fire at the Battle of the Aisne on 16th September causing nearly 100 casualties. From these one officer and 12 men were killed and to make matters worse, atrocious cold and wet weather conditions caused a sick list of 60. Once more in combat during the so called 'Race to the Sea' in late October at Givenchy they again suffered another 100 casualties. Therefore, within a matter of weeks this battalion alone in two 'minor' actions suffered nearly 200 casualties[12]. Also, arriving in France at the beginning of November the 2nd Devons had just under 20 casualties from enemy action and by the end of the month, also because of the weather over 70 men sick, mainly with frostbite. A month later in one, so called 'minor' action near Neuve Chapelle, they suffered three officers killed and five wounded while the other rank's casualties were 121 killed, wounded and missing[13].

To this I suggest can be added the earlier idea that *'It will be over by Christmas'*. As we have seen above most governments initially believed this, therefore transcending to recruiters promoting the idea. It is easy to understand that too many volunteers it was obvious 'the more men we have the quicker the victory'. Patriotism, adventure, peer pressure, 'the only thing to do' or boredom convinced these men, hence the early enthusiasm and for some praying that it wouldn't be over before they experienced what they believed war to be. But of course Christmas 1914 came and went and there were to be three more Yuletides and nearly a fourth before that optimistic notion came to fruition. After receiving the terrible news of high casualty rates the war continued to shock. Therefore potential volunteers could ask themselves what enormous effect, if they volunteered and were injured or killed, would this cause to their own families. Also, by extension, those small communities to which they belonged?

A Different outlook?

My assessment is that even though recruiting in the West Country from 1914 to January 1916 could appear different than other areas but this, in my opinion is not the case. It could be interpreted as lower but this is because of statistics as it had less population density. Unquestionably the regional system, as arranged geographically, took no account of recruiting figures between rural counties and mass centres that provided the majority of the volunteers. Latter examples being the Birmingham nexus in the Midlands or the northern Northumberland-Tyneside area or the Clyde-Forth conurbations in Southern Scotland[14].

These areas had far greater populations when compared to those with far smaller populations such as Devon and Cornwall whose men and later women did serve in all areas of that terrible conflict. In support of the above we must look at the obvious willingness of those of both counties as both the Naval and Army Reserves to go to war, plus the men of the Territorial Wessex Division who had gone to India, as in small communities their departure counted very significantly but less overall statistically. This I hazard supports the idea that nothing more was needed and they had already 'done their bit', [see above The Cornishman, Tuesday 24th September and the Cornish Guardian 2nd October 1914] therefore, in their minds, they had fulfilled their obligation and further volunteering was not required. In fact as we have seen previously the document that supports these ideas show that the casualties suffered in Devon and Cornwall by its Royal Marine and Royal Navy servicemen were nearly four times higher than the national average. This emphasises the fact that these maritime counties also provided hundreds of young and older men in boats and ships carrying essential men, supplies and foodstuffs thus risking their lives against an ever growing U-Boat presence.

If we put everything together there was but little, if any, difference in attitude when it came to volunteer recruitment from other like counties or areas. So therefore when it comes to enlisting for military service, overall they were alike, ordinary people in kingdom united in attitude towards the war.

I will add that, for those Britons who had not volunteered the later increase of wages caused by staff shortages on the land and in the war industries initially led to a betterment of their situation. However, as the war continued wages in many sectors did not keep up with increasing food prices as the cost of living increased. When compared to August 1914 it rose by about 17 per cent by December of that year and 65 per cent by July 1916[15.] But by then many could not volunteer, as the war dragged on their services in the mines or factories, fields or on the sea were needed to keep Britain fed and its war time industries in production. At that time we were fortunate as a 'nation in arms' that we were sensible enough to call on that most inestimable asset, women who earned their place as valuable members in all areas of the workforce.

Conscription finally did lead to a feeling of everyone being involved as, in a sense, they also 'Dug In'. Although those civilians on what is now termed the Home Front were dealing with shortages of just about everything, they were working to back up not only their sons, brothers, fathers and friends fighting or in the transport or medical services but also their female relatives, on a 'front'.

By 1918 the outcome relied on the young, but well trained, 19 to 20 year olds many of whom bore the final awful burden on the Western Front as shown in photographs of the final '100 days'. For civilians admittedly there was confrontation with authority at times of stress. But ultimately a more united British people, finally The United Kingdom, together with its allies, and the United States did not lose the war for democracy. It helped liberate occupied areas of France, Belgium and Luxemburg from the cruel invader[16].

APPENDIX ONE

Cornwall VCs

Horace Augustus Curtis VC was born in 1891 at St Anthony on the Roseland Peninsula, Cornwall. Originally a worker in the china clay industry he volunteered for the DCLI but was transferred to the Royal Dublin Fusiliers. On 18 October 1918 the then Sergeant Curtis, 2nd Battalion Royal Dublin Fusiliers fought in an action near Le Cateau that earned him the Victoria Cross. His citation reads:

> *No.14107 Sjt. Horace Augustus Curtis. 2nd Battalion, R. Dub. Fusiliers.*
>
> *For most conspicuous bravery and devotion to duty East of Le Cateau on the morning of 18th October 1918, when in attack his platoon came unexpectedly under intense machine-gun fire. Realising that the attack would fail unless the enemy guns were silenced, Sgt. Curtis, without hesitation, rushed forward through our own barrage and the enemy fire and killed and wounded the teams of two of the guns, whereupon the remaining four guns surrendered. Then turning his attention to a train-load of reinforcements, he succeeded in capturing over 100 of the enemy before his comrades joined him. His valour and disregard of danger inspired all.*
>
> *The London Gazette* (Supplement). 4 January 1919. p. 307.

In his book, *Orange, Green and Khaki* Tom Johnstone writes that having located the machine gun and receiving covering fire from his platoon Sergeant Curtis outflanked the position and bombed (hand grenades) it to surrender. Advancing further he came across a train and after shooting the driver virtually captured the train load of troops before his men joined him. Among the booty captured by the Dublins that day was an entire battery of guns, complete with horse teams. He notes that a Sergeant Robert Downie who, earlier in the war, had also been awarded a VC joined Curtis in his platoon which he estimated was probably unique to the BEF[1].

After the war Horace Curtis returned to Cornwall and according to his relations spoke very rarely of his war service or the acts of bravery for which he was awarded his VC. He died in Redruth, Cornwall in 1968.

Ernest Herbert Pitcher VC, DSM was born on the 31st December 1881 at Mullion, Cornwall and aged 15 years joined the Royal Navy.

At the outbreak of the conflict he was serving in the Dreadnought *HMS King George V,* transferring to a Special Service Branch Q ship in 1915 commanded by Commander Gordon Campbell. Q Ships were heavily armed vessels disguised as 'false-flag' merchantman, designed to lure enemy submarines to surface and then engage them with gunfire or torpedoes.

In this they were successful as *HMS Farnborough (Q.5)* sank two U-boats; but was herself sunk by the second, with the now Captain Campbell being awarded the VC after this second action. Most of the crew, including Pitcher, were rescued and followed Campbell to *HMS Pargust.*

On the 7th June 1917 *Pargust* sank the U-boat UC-29 but was herself severely damaged. The Admiralty decided that *Pargust's* action was worthy of the VC but that all of the crew had acted with equal valour, so article 13 of the VC's royal warrant was applied and the ship's company voted for one commissioned officer and one petty officer or seaman to receive the award: consequently these were the ship's First Lieutenant, Ronald Stuart and Seaman William Williams. On this occasion Pitcher received the Distinguished Service Medal. Captain Campbell and the crew then transferred to *HMS Dunraven,* in which the action took place for which Pitcher was awarded the VC[2].

His citation reads:

On the 8th August, 1917, H.M.S. "Dunraven," under the command of Captain Gordon Campbell, V.C., D.S.O., R.N., sighted an enemy submarine [UC-71] on the horizon. In her role of armed British merchant ship, the "Dunraven" continued her zig-zag course, whereupon the submarine closed, remaining submerged to within 5,000 yards, and then, rising to the surface, opened fire. The "Dunraven" returned the fire with her merchant ship gun, at the same time reducing speed to enable the enemy to overtake her. Wireless signals were also sent out for the benefit of the submarine: "Help! come quickly – submarine chasing and shelling me." Finally, when the shells began falling close, the "Dunraven" stopped and abandoned ship by the "panic party." [The "panic party" was a small number of men who were to "abandon ship" during an attack to continue the impersonation of a merchant ship.] The ship was then being heavily shelled, and on fire aft. In the meantime the submarine closed to 400 yards distant, partly obscured from view by the dense clouds of smoke issuing from the "Dunraven's" stern. Despite the knowledge that the after magazine must inevitably explode if he waited, and further, that a gun and gun's crew lay concealed over the magazine, Captain Campbell decided to reserve his fire until the submarine had passed clear of the smoke. A moment later, however, a heavy explosion occurred aft, blowing the gun and gun's crew into the air, and accidentally starting the fire-gongs at the remaining gun positions; screens were immediately dropped, and the only gun that would bear opened fire, but the submarine, apparently frightened by the explosion, had already commenced to submerge. Realising that a torpedo must inevitably follow, Captain Campbell ordered the surgeon to remove all wounded and conceal them in cabins; hoses were also turned on the poop, which was a mass of flames. A signal was sent out warning men-of-war to divert all traffic below the horizon in order that nothing should interrupt the final phase of the action. Twenty minutes later a torpedo again struck the ship abaft the engine-room. An additional party of men were again sent away as a "panic party," and left the ship to outward appearances completely abandoned, with the White Ensign flying and guns unmasked. For the succeeding fifty minutes the submarine examined the ship through her periscope. During this period boxes of cordite and shells exploded every few minutes, and the fire on the poop still blazed furiously. Captain Campbell and the handful of officers and men who remained on board lay hidden during this ordeal. The submarine then rose to the surface astern, where no guns could bear and shelled the ship closely for twenty minutes. The enemy then submerged and steamed past the ship 150 yards off, examining her through the periscope. Captain Campbell decided then to fire one of his torpedoes, but missed by a few inches. The submarine crossed the bows and came slowly down the other side, whereupon a second torpedo was fired and missed again. The enemy observed it and immediately submerged. Urgent signals for assistance were immediately sent out, but pending arrival of assistance Captain Campbell arranged for a third "panic party" to jump overboard if necessary and leave one gun's crew on board for a final attempt to destroy the enemy, should he again attack. Almost immediately afterwards, however, British and American destroyers arrived on the scene, the wounded were transferred, boats were recalled and the fire extinguished. The "Dunraven" although her stern was awash, was taken in tow, but the weather grew worse, and early the following morning she sank with colours flying.

The London Gazette (Supplement). 20 November 1918. p. 13694.

The bravery of the men manning the Q ships is self apparent with the award of eight VCs during the war to various ships crews. As with all clandestine and submarine warfare operations however, there had also been the subject of accusations from both sides as to the lack of humanity and the breaking of the Rules of War. After the sinking of the liner the *SS Lusitania* in May 1915 with the deaths of 1201 men, women and children the German propaganda machine actually produced a special medal in celebration. On the 19th of August Commander Godfrey Herbert's Q ship *HMS Baralong* sank the submarine *U27* whose survivors had then gone to a neutral US cargo vessel. He sent his Royal Marine contingent onto the ship where they hunted and shot all of the German survivors as he was worried, his report stated, that they would destroy the cargo[3].

Whether Commander Herbert needs defending or not, it should be remembered that these men came from the Victorian/Edwardian period and who did however, at least profess, that killing women and children was complete anathema. Also, following the sinking of the *Lusitania* another passenger vessel the *SS Arabic* was sunk by U24 causing the death of 44 passengers and in just one month four U boats had sunk 35 vessels killing 78 sailors and passengers[4].

For information Q is for Queenstown, now Cobh in the Irish Republic, that, during the Great War, was the location of the RN HQ for the Western Approaches.

James Henry Finn V.C. was born in 1893 at St Clement, Truro, Cornwall. His father, John Finn, served in the Duke of Cornwall's Light Infantry in the Boer War and again in the Special Reserve during the First World War. James Finn served as a Territorial soldier with the 5th Battalion, DCLI before moving to the South Wales Valleys looking for work. He eventually found employment at the colliery at Cwmtillery near Abertillery.

On the outbreak of war, he immediately enlisted with the local regiment, the South Wales Borderers and was duly posted to their 4th (Service) Battalion[5]. On enlistment, his surname was incorrectly recorded as "Fynn"(see below)

On 15 July 1915, the battalion landed at Gallipoli. Finn was wounded in the knee and chest, and invalided back to Britain. After the withdrawal from Gallipoli, the battalion had moved to Mesopotamia, and Finn rejoined them there. He acted as orderly to the commanding officer, Lt. Col. C. E. Kitchen

His citation reads:

> *It was on 9 April 1916 at Sanna-i-Yat, Mesopotamia (now Iraq), that 22-year-old Private Fynn earned the Victoria Cross for most conspicuous bravery. After a night attack he was one of a small party which dug-in in front of our advanced line and about 300 yards from the enemy's trenches. Seeing several wounded men lying out in front he went out and bandaged them all under heavy fire, making several journeys in order to do so. He then went back to our advanced trench for a stretcher and, being unable to get one, he himself carried on his back a badly wounded man into safety. He then returned and, aided by another man who was wounded during the act, carried in another badly wounded man. He was under continuous fire while performing this gallant work.*

The London Gazette (Supplement). 22 June 1916. p. 9418.

The award of the VC followed action at Sanna-i-yat a battle that to me sums up the blind incompetence and complacent ignorance of the enemy displayed by many of the senior British commanders. This includes the C-in-C General Charles Townsend during the Mesopotamia campaign in general and the attempt to relieve him and the Imperial forces besieged in Kut-al-Amara. It is worth quoting verbatim the opinion of Brigadier General Fraser, commenting on his commander's (Lt. General Goringe) talents after the abortive attack at Sanna-i-yat on the 5th April 1916, said *"His cursed optimism, contempt for the Turks, contempt for the principles of war and for the lessons of this war, have again landed us in failure and run up a butcher's bill. This is culpable homicide[6]."* What had seemed initially to be 'a piece of cake' eventually cost 1,868 casualties[7].

Added to the problems of the wounded was the dire lack of medical facilities; and the issue here goes right to the very top. Two weeks before the attack Whitehall had contacted the Viceroy of India Lord Harding asking if the army needed help from the Red Cross, to which he replied *'Nothing required at present. If anything is needed in future, will not hesitate to ask you'*, which amounted to criminal neglect[8].

APPENDIX TWO

Devon VCs

<u>Thomas Henry Sage V.C.</u> was born in Tiverton, Devon, England on the 8th December 1882. While a Private in the 8th Battalion, The Somerset Light Infantry (Prince Albert's) he was awarded the Victoria Cross. His award citation reads:

On 4 October 1917 at Tower Hamlets Spur, east of Ypres, Belgium, Private Sage was in a shell-hole with eight other men, one of whom was shot while throwing a bomb which fell back into the shell-hole. Private Sage, with great presence of mind, immediately threw himself on it, and so saved the lives of several of his comrades, although he himself was severely wounded.

The London Gazette (Supplement). 30433 14 December 1917. p.13223.

Tower Hamlets is a a low ridge just south of the Menin Road and just west of the village of Gheluvelt the buildings within which by 1917 consisted of levelled ruins. The term had been given earlier during the fighting for the Ypres Salient by the British who had difficulty with most foreign – to them – names i.e. Ploegsteert Wood became Plugstreet Wood and Ypres, Wipers. Irreverence has always been a part of the make-up of the humour generated by the British so, for example the French General Franchet d'Esperey became 'Desperate Franky'.

The 8th (Service) Battalion. 63rd Brigade, 37th Division went into action on the 4th October 1917 during what is now termed The Battle of Broodseinde during the 3rd Battle of Ypres. Their attack concentrated on the area around the Menin Road that had been previously heavily shelled *'the general line* (trench) *running about 150 yards west of the road owing to the previous shelling of the area the road was no longer a landmark'*[1]. The attack commenced at 6am accompanied by artillery but *'the curtain of fire appeared very thin'.* The German held their positions tenaciously taking a heavy toll on the attackers from machine guns and hand grenades creating the incident that resulted in the award of the VC to Thomas Sage as the citation states. At the end of the day casualties had been very high with three officers killed, three wounded, 27 other ranks killed, 74 wounded and a further 12 were missing.

The battalion consolidated its gains by occupying various fixed positions in this lunar like landscape instead of a fixed trench line and one such, No.4 Post, contained 12 men when on the night of the 14th it was attacked. One man survived and told his officers that the enemy had shot the wounded men without mercy and that he had only lived because he 'played dead'. This enraged the battalion and consequently it was reported in the history of the regiment that when the British heavy artillery shelled the Germans opposite the following day *'The great shells blew posts and emplacements to pieces, and trench traverses, debris and the bodies of mangled Germans shot up into the air to the delight of the Somerset men, who had suffered at the hands of the enemy. It is admitted that all war is horrible but it is necessary. The shooting of the wounded in "No.4 Post" was the work of savage brutes and not soldiers'²*.

Theodore Bayley Hardy, V.C., DSO, MC was born in Exeter, Devon, England on the 20 October 1863. He was a British Army chaplain and one of the most decorated non-combatants of the First World War.

His VC award citation reads:

> *For conspicuous gallantry and devotion to duty in volunteering to go with a rescue party for some men who had been left stuck in the mud the previous night between the enemy's outpost line and our own. All the men except one were brought in. He then organised a party for the rescue of this man, and remained with it all night, though under rifle-fire at close range, which killed one of the party. With his left arm in splints, owing to a broken wrist, and under the worst weather conditions, he crawled out with patrols to within seventy yards of the enemy and remained with wounded men under heavy fire.*

The London Gazette (Supplement).30561 5 March 1918. pp. 2895–2896.

It is difficult not to be cynical about the role of religion in the First World War. At a time when Western Christianity perceived itself as a force within European countries and preached the peaceful tenets of that faith there was no rush by the vast majority of the established religions to prevent or condemn the conflict – far from it.

In 1914, at least 30 million (or near 90% of the total population) professed a Christian religion in the British Isles. Yet most church leaders fully endorsed the government's declaration of war against a fellow Christian country.

There were 117 chaplains in the pre-war army. By 1918 there were 1,985 Church of England chaplains, 649 Roman Catholic and about another thousand from the smaller Wesleyan, Baptist, Methodist, Congregationalist, Presbyterian and Salvation Army, Protestant denominations, plus sixteen from the Jewish faith. The religious believed that the conflict would revitalise a spirituality evidently lacking in the majority who, it was felt, gave worship only lip service. This "crusade" against the evils of German militarism would be endorsed by God: as the convinced cleric Bishop of London Arthur Winnington-Ingram put it, *"a great crusade – we cannot deny it – to kill Germans. To kill them, not for the sake of killing but to save the world ..."*

Imperial Germany had come via war and political intrigue to creation in 1871 after a successful Prussian conflict with France. Like all other countries involved in the conflict, they believed that God was on their side, hence "Gott Mit Uns" *("God with us")* stamped on the belt buckle of every Prussian (but not German) infantryman. Prussia was the biggest state of this Empire and had a majority of people who were rather militant Protestants; consequently it had an uneasy religious relationship with the Catholic Church and therefore with its next biggest partner, Bavaria. Here, although its citizens gave political allegiance to the Empire, about 70% gave their religious support to the Pope, and consequently felt that they were discriminated against by their dominant neighbour.

Conflict, it was anticipated, would eliminate such perceived divisions and provide both a political and religious unity, with the Kaiser declaring after the start of hostilities that "Ich kenne keine Parteien mehr, ich kenne nur noch Deutsche!" *("I know no more parties, I know only Germans!")*. Patriotic fervor ran high with the popular slogan "Gott strafe England" *(May God Punish England)* and its extension, the poem *"Hymn of Hate"*, ironically both created by the German Jew Ernst Lissauer who later fled to the UK after the rise of the Nazis, but in 1914 he was as emotional and as aggressive as the Bishop of London had been in supporting his country's efforts to win. We see here that, for some, strife was a chance to show loyalty to the state and brought sought-for endorsements to minorities, however, this sentiment was rejected by the majority of his religion.

Its ally Austria-Hungary was a fractious empire divided, however, more along ethnic rather than religious disunity and its history over many hundreds of years had given it experience that forced it to take notice of minority political and religious rights – as long as this did not threaten the unity of the state. A more rural entity, generally the beliefs of its soldiers were more unquestioning than those of more industrialised societies and its attempts at a homogeneous state is reflected by its armed forces who contained chaplains of the majority Roman Catholic faith and also those of the Greek Catholic, Greek Orthodox, Protestant Lutherans and Calvinists denominations plus Muslim clerics and, in time of war, Jewish Rabbis.

Interestingly, as with the other belligerents, these men echoed the patriotic ethos of their nation, as remembered by Lt General Sandor Pavai: "the good old army chaplains were always there to strengthen soldiers' spirit, before and during the fight, in the trenches, in the attacks ..."

These are just three examples of the conundrum of how hundreds of convinced men, imbued with a high moral sense to God, their religion and of service to their fellow man, served within their armed forces. Many displayed understandable human weakness if not fear and hypocrisy, were reported to have disappeared, so it seemed, when battle commenced; however, some were extremely brave: three Victoria Crosses and numerous other awards for valour were given by the British alone.

On all sides pastors, chaplains and padres, monks, imams and rabbis helped the wounded, rescued the injured and even, it is recorded, occasionally joined in the fight. On reflection, they seem within their own small sphere, to represent the majority, caught unawares and trying to make sense of this Great War[3].

Richard Douglas Sandford V.C. was born in Exeter, Devon, England
on 11 May 1891 the son of Venerable Ernest Grey Sandford, Archdeacon of Exeter. He was a Royal Navy officer and his award citation reads:

This officer was in command of Submarine C3 and most skillfully placed that vessel in between the piles of the viaduct before lighting his fuse and abandoning her. He eagerly undertook this hazardous enterprise, although well aware (as were his crew) that if the means of rescue failed he or any of his crew were in the water at the moment of the explosion, they would have been killed outright by the force of such an explosion. Yet Lieutenant Sandford disdained to use the gyro steering, which would have enabled him and his crew to abandon the submarine at a safe distance, and preferred to make sure, as far as was humanly possible, of the accomplishment of his duty.

The London Gazette, (Supplement). 3087 19th July 1918. p 8585

Most people who visit the beautiful town of Bruges in Belgium do not realise that this provided the base for a major part of the German U Boat fleet during WW1. The town is connected to two Belgium North Sea ports firstly Ostend by an 11 mile long canal and Zeebrugge by a shorter seven mile canal, access to the sea from both laying beyond massively powerful lock gates, as they do to this day. There had been various plans put forward to reduce the effectiveness of the U Boat campaign by attacking the ports including one using poison gas but never acted upon because of the concern about deaths to the civilian Belgian population.

One part of the justification for the Third Battle of Ypres, better known by the ominous name Passchendaele, put forward by Field Marshall Haig and given powerful support by the First Sea Lord, Admiral Jellicoe involved the capture of the two ports and Bruges by clearing the Flanders coast[4].

The Ypres Campaign resulted in failure and losses to shipping remained significantly high. For example previously in six months the monthly loses from submarine action had more than trebled to 368,521 tons but U Boat loses, for example during the whole of 1916 amounted to 25 including four to accidents and five to action by our Russian ally[5] - 'something had to be done' resulting in Operation ZO, the seaborne attacks against Zeebrugge and Ostend. Zeebrugge had a very long sea mole to protect the port that was heavily defended by fixed artillery positions and infantry emplacements. One part of the very ambitious plan to block the ports with ships placed in position and then sunk across its entrance involved placing a submarine against the metal pier connecting the concrete mole to the mainland and blowing it up therefore destroying part of the structure so isolating the garrison. Volunteers were asked for and Lieutenant Richard Sandford offered his services.

As planned his part of the operation was a success as is recorded in his citation. However, as with previous attempts to block a harbour by sinking ships in the approach did not have the planned outcome because the Germans quickly altered the ships locations so their operations suffered a mere interruption and not cessation. The similar attack against Ostend was a complete failure so much so that a second attempt was made shortly after but again with little success.

It should be added that because of high casualties[6] to the Allies* of 227 killed and 356 wounded and the less than adequate results these events still cause controversy and spirited argument to this day. I add that German casualties were amazingly small with just eight German naval personnel killed[7].

As was to be expected in such an audacious action, including Lieutenant Sandford, eight V.C.s were awarded split equally between the RN and the Royal Marines plus 17 DSOs, 28 DSCs, 16 CGMs and 139 DSMs[8].

Unfortunately, Richard Sandford V.C. died of typhoid fever just 12 days after the signing of the Armistice on the 23rd of November 1918.

* The French Navy contributed eight TBDs and four motor boats, but saw no action. The Royal Australian Navy one officer and ten men. Page 306 in the above.

Although we celebrate the cessation of hostilities on the 11th of November 1918 for some the conflict continued as 10 days later Britain dispatched a small naval force to the Baltic. This happened after a request had been received from the newly independent state of Estonia to assist its fight against Soviet forces. One of the Royal Navy officers with the force was

Lieutenant Gordon Charles Steele V.C. who was born in Exeter, Devon, England on 1 November 1891. His award citation reads:

> *On 18 August 1919 at Kronstadt, Russia, Lieutenant Steele was second-in-command of Coastal Motor Boat 88. Steele's boat became illuminated by an enemy searchlight. Very heavy machine gun fire followed immediately, the Captain being killed and the boat thrown off course. A British aircraft saw the problem, dived on the searchlight and put it out with gunfire. Lieutenant Steele took the wheel and steadied the boat, lifting the dead officer away from the steering and firing position, and successfully torpedoed the battleship Andrei Pervozvanny at 100 yards range. He then maneuvered the CMB in a very confined space to get a clear shot at the other Battleship Petropavlovsk before making for the safety of the bay.*

The London Gazette (Supplement). 21 October 1919. p.12979.

The Thorneycroft designed Coastal Motor Boat such as CMB 88 were extremely fast, capable of 35 to 40 knots (44mph) 55 feet in length and normally carried a crew of three to five, latter models could be armed with two torpedoes, four depth charges and several light machine guns[9]. A previous attack in June 1919 against a Soviet cruiser using such a vessel had resulted in its sinking. The British recognised that for their mission to succeed an attack on the main Soviet naval base should be attempted. Consequently an audacious plan was hatched to attack the ships and dry dock in the well defended Kronstadt harbour by a much larger force of CMBs. However, after a great deal of training using buoys to represent the ships and the inner dimensions of the port it was apparent that the mission would be extremely difficult[10], but it was considered of such importance that the attack went ahead during the night of the 18th of August with air support.

The plan involved eight CMBs and eight aircraft from the RAF base at Koivisto, Finland with Commander Agar who had attacked and sunk the cruiser in June, his role now being to oversee and lead, while the other seven CMBs were all armed, bar one, with two torpedoes.

Unfortunately, one broke down and therefore the plan proceeded with the now six boats attacking in two waves of three with 11 weapons.

It must be pointed out that confusion must have reigned. What exactly happened at night in a well defended harbour with an attack mounted by fragile, fast boats that were being fired on could never be known exactly.

As planned the RAF were already attacking the port with bombs and machine guns, sending the defender running to safety when the naval attack commenced at 0140hrs as the first wave entered the harbour at high speed. A submarine depot ship the *Pamyat Azova*, after being hit by CMB 79's one torpedo capsized and as the CMB manoeuvred to leave the harbour moments later the battleship *Andrie Pervozvanni* was then hit on the bow by two fired by *CMB 31* and began flooding. It was at this moment that the garrison's gunners regained their positions and began firing on the attackers, unfortunately, hitting the commander of CMB 88 Lieutenant Dayrell-Reed who sustained a very serious head wound from which he later died. The second in command Lieutenant Steele immediately took over and fired one torpedo at the Pervozanni and moments later at another battleship the *Petropavlovsk* with his two weapons hitting both[11]. Outside, as it manoeuvred to attack, the guard ship *Gavrill* now opened fire destroying CMB 24. Further tragedy took place when upon leaving the base one of the second wave violently collided with CMB 79 with both then being destroyed by Russian fire.

The action resulted in all three Russian ships sunk or disabled but also 10 RN personnel had been killed and nine captured plus, as we have seen, the loss of three CMBs. Only one of the British boats escaped unscathed.

In his book *Warships in the Baltic Campaign 1918 - 20* the writer Angus Konstam states that the resulting Soviet demoralization after the attack resulted in their other ships hardly ever leaving port for the rest of the campaign; the exception being its very effective submarines, though the loss of the *Pamyat Azova* must have had a reduction in their overall ability. However, elsewhere he also points out that because the Soviets concentrated their efforts on supplying men and material to the army, therefore, to the detriment of its navy, plus the lack of competent and experienced officers to manage such complicated weaponry as a battleship, surely might well be an even greater reason for inactivity. As an example of the reduction of numbers Commissar Stalin was driving the Red Army into Azerbaijan with Soviet Marines operating in the Caspian Sea[12] nearly 2000 miles from Kronstadt.

The raid was carried out 'in the best traditions of the service' becoming one of the most highly decorated operations in British military history. Of the 55 participants in the sea and air no less that 48 received an award[13] including two Victoria Crosses[14].

However all was not well with the mission as troubles had broken out on board a number of British ships as some of the minesweeping crews refused duty and there was also a minor mutiny and even trouble on the flagship the cruiser HMS Delhi. The causes were pay and conditions, a longing for discharge at war's end, indifferent food and a poor system of leave allocation. Partly as a result of these disturbances and partly because of Government policy the Baltic fleet was run down during the Spring of 1920[15].

The campaign had cost the British 127 men killed and seen the loss of two destroyers, a submarine, two sloops, seven CMBs and a store carrier.

Was it worth it? We know that the Communist/Soviet took over the majority of the old Russian Empire; however, because of the (mainly) British presence and commitment the three Baltic States of Lithuania, Estonia and Latvia and by extension Finland remained independent.

It should be noted that Mr Konstam's book[16] concerning the August attack on Kronstadt still shows great bravery by all concerned but possibly because of the nature of the attack, a different story as to that in the citation.

APPENDIX THREE

The evolution of the battlefield rifle

There had been a revolution during the just over 100 years in firearm technology. Within this I include not only the rifle or hand held weapons but also the projectiles that they fired. If you look at 1815 the Battle of Waterloo all of the weapons used required very careful handling and multiple actions to enable the holder to load.

The musket projected a round lead ball by the use of gunpowder with the soldier using a pre-prepared paper cartridge with a twist at the top that contained the powder and ball. The man had to tear this paper twist off with the weapon in an upright position and pour the contents down the barrel.

The musket came with a ram rod attached below the wooden stock that had a flared, button shaped end. The soldier now pulled out the rod and rammed it with some force down the barrel to secure and compact the powder and ball together. This part of the sequence complete the weapon could be brought to around waist height ensuring of course that it never pointed down to ensure no disruption of the load as, in extreme cases, through fear or inexperience, the ball could and did roll out. On the musket's right side and bolted to it, another part of the firing mechanism had been installed that consisted of several metal moving parts. A lid that covered a small flat shallow pan and an upright, spring-loaded 'cock' that contained a flint. This was now pulled back, the top of the pan swivelled and loose powder shaken into it.

The weapon could now be fired by pulling the trigger located again below the stock, this being attached by the spring to the 'cock'.

Although the famed Baker Rifle in the hands of the uniquely trained British 95th Rifle Regiment and possibly, on special occasions, the ordinary musket could be used while lying down, for the great majority, training ensured that combat occurred while standing. All loose gunpowder weapons created a great deal of smoke; consequently most early battlefield fighting conditions must have been fought in a sulphurous mist until blown away by wind; however, as can be imagined during too high windy or wet weather this often made firing impossible.

The pistol used the same firing mechanism; however, they did not have the cartridge. Loading a smaller weapon with loose powder and ball must have been consequently easier but these again would still be affected by adverse weather conditions.

All Governments become parsimonious when war's end and Britain's did exactly this with further development that now evolved into the percussion cap activation instead of the pan and flint, but still using the same musket. This ensured that in wet or windy conditions the weapons could still fire, but ram rod, ball and gunpowder still produced the same smoke-filled conditions.

Advances in science accelerated research into the greater efficiency -killing power- of armies as smokeless propellant and the self contained cartridge. This combined by the early start of the 20th century with magazine rifles, where five or ten bullets could be stored and then brought up into a breach activated by a 'bolt action' ready to fire. This brought greater range, accuracy and a soldier so equipped who could stand, lie down or even lay on his back, without worrying if his weapon could fire when needed[1]. It also brought an 'explosive' effect if hitting bone on the recipient when the bullet struck them.

The British it must be remembered had fought against an enemy equipped (The Boers) with bolt action, magazine rifles, mainly the rightly famed German Gewehr G98 Mauser. This had a calibre of 7.92mm and magazine with a capacity of five rounds. It weighed 4.14kg and had an overall length, without bayonet of 1255mm.

The British at this period fielded the British Lee-Metford Mk1, calibre .303 inches (7.69mm) with a magazine containing eight bullets, that weighed 4.37kg and had an overall length without bayonet of 1257mm. By 1900 - 1902 this had changed to the well known Lee-Enfield Mk1 that nearly matched the statistics of the Mauser that the German army was equipped except for a magazine with 10 rounds.

It is somewhat ironic that the Belgian army of 1914 that put up such unexpected resistance to the German invasion adapted and then manufactured a version of the Mauser Rifle in 1889. This did have the five round magazine but with a slightly smaller round of 7.65mm, an overall length of 1295mm and weighed 4.01kg. Also the French army used a bolt action rifle – The 1886 Lebel, calibre 8mm with an eight round magazine which measured 1295mm and weighed 4.28kg. As the French army believed and trained to achieve attack without pause – a'outrance – the fixed bayonet was always attached during the early part of the war, a style of aggression that caused horrendous casualties to its men from German firepower[2].

Possible use of the 'Dum – Dum' Bullet?

As this type of ammunition creates appalling wounds it is disturbing to read the British Medical Journal of 19th December 1896 that celebrates the invention of the Dum-Dum bullet in that British Indian Ammunition Factory. This fact allows the right of the German enemy of 1914 to be suspicious of our weaponry. Although it is generally discounted now that the Germans thought the British were using machine guns instead of rifles at the battle of Mons in 1914 it is true that the latter were well trained in the use of the weapon, producing high volumes of fire when ordered to do so. Unfortunately for the Germans during these early battles they experienced very high casualty rates and were nearly overwhelmed by the number of their own wounded. Because of this on many occasions little medical attention, or even food were given to injured prisoners of war, for example, those of the Royal Irish Regiment in October 1914. When these men were finally removed to a rear medical unit they unfortunately fell under the 'care' of its commander, an extremely angry German doctor. This physician wrongly accused the British in general and these men specifically of using 'Dum-Dum' ammunition, which had been specifically banned by the *1899 Hague Declaration* – '*The Geneva Convention*', claiming that this had been created after copying a diagram found in a German newspaper. This type of bullet, he stated, must be causing the 'explosive' wounds for which his unit were treating German soldiers and as a result felt justified in refusing the Irish soldiers little if any medical attention, thankfully, one German doctor at the facility defied this order and treated the most badly injured.

In late 1914 prior to the German's setting up research to prove such a claim, their Government made an official complaint both to the Red Cross and the neutral United States in a telegram from Kaiser Wilhelm to President Woodrow Wilson. It claimed that the British were using machines to manufacture this type of ammunition in Belgium and then using it in combat. However, their own later medical research undertaken by Professor Dr. M. Kirchener, the Senior Surgeon of the 3rd Bavarian Army Corps proved this was unfounded. The Professor wrote that although his government claimed to have found such machines in Belgium for these illegal bullets manufacture there was no conclusive medical evidence to support this. '*Extensive destruction of the tissues, particularly large and lacerated wounds of entry and exit, do not of themselves afford proof of a dumdum bullet; they occur rather with the use of the regular infantry bullet*'. He went on '*If bones are involved, the resultant action may be due to the usual explosive action of the regular bullet at close range*'. It was, noted Lt. Col. E.M. Pilcher DSO of the British Royal Army Medical Corps, a fair presentation of the comparative effects of the modern pointed, composite rifle ammunition and of the so-called Dum-Dum bullet.

Such were the horrific wounds created all governments involved in the conflict complained that the enemy were manufacturing and using such bullets throughout the war although this was never sanctioned or proven[3].

Though, as it was so easy to achieve it is possible that a minority of combatants on both sides did modify ammunition by flattening or drilling a hole at the conical end, such is the hatred that warfare engenders[4].

REFERENCES

Chapter One
A history of Volunteering

[1]   https://www.researchgate.net/figure/Literacy-in-England-1580-1920_fig3_228553349

[2]   Wilson, A.N. 2002 'The Victorians' Arrow Books p363

[3]   Jackson, Tabitha 1999 'The Boer War' 4 books p80

[4]   Parkyn, Major H.G. 1936'English Militia Regiments' Journal of the Society for Army Historical Research Vol. 15, No. 60. P216

[5]   Holmes, Richard 2011. 'Soldiers' Harper Press pp94-95

[6]   Ibid p95

[7]   Bennet, Mark 2018 'Portrayals of the British Militia, 1852–1916' Historical Research OUP p334

[8]   Sleigh, Arthur 1850 'The Royal Militia and Yeomanry' British Army Dispatch Press p xv

[9]   Clarke, I.F. 1995 'The Tale of the Next War 1871-1914. L.U.P. p14

[10]   Beckett, Ian F.W.2007 'Riflemen Form' A study of the rifle volunteer movement 1859 to 1908' Pen & Sword p7

[11]   Ibid p8

[12]   Ibid p8

[13]   Ibid p7

[14]   HC Deb 07 May 1852 vol 121 cc371-413

[15]   Holmes, Richard 2005' Tommy' Harper Perennial p123

[16]   Holmes, Richard 2011 'Soldiers' Harper Press p100

[17]   Westlake, Ray 2019'A Guide to the Volunteers of England' N&M p 3

[18]   Ibid p3

[19]   Beckett, Ian 2007 'Riflemen Form. A study of the rifle volunteer movement 1859 to 1908' Pen &Sword p54&55

[20]   Ibid p52

[21]   May, R & Embleton, G 1975 'The Franco-Prussian War 1870' p60

[22]   Chesney, George '1871' Dodo Press

[23]   Beckett, Ian 2007 'Riflemen Form. A study of the rifle volunteer movement 1859 to 1908' Pen &Sword pp54-56

24 Ibid p133

25 Clarke, I.F. 1995 The Tale of the Next Great War 1871-1914 L.U.P p16

26 Peacock, Dr A 2006 'From the Vale to the Veldt'. G.H.Smith p299

27 Beckett, Ian 2007 'Riflemen Form. A study of the rifle volunteer movement 1859 to 1908' Pen &Sword pp231 – 246

28 Messenger, Charles 2005 'Call to Arms' Cassel p91

29 Bloomfield, Peter 2006 'The Gloucester Archives' p12

30 Holmes, Richard 2011 'Soldiers' Harper Press p104

31 Owen, Brian, 1979 'The Worcestershire Yeomanry Cavalry' Worcester Museum p4

32 Ibid p7

33 Royal Cornwall Gazette. Friday 17th April 1840

34 Holmes, Richard. 2011 'Soldiers' Harper Press p107

35 Rowe, John 'The North Devon Yeomanry' Barnstaple Museum p14

36 Hay, George '2017 'The Yeomanry and the State' Palgrave Macmillan (pdf) pp109-112

Chapter Two
"Gentlemen Now Abed?"

1 Trew, Peter 1999 'The Boer War Generals' Sutton Publishing p7

2 Packenham, Thomas 1988 'The Boer War' Futura pp76-77

3 Jackson, Tabitha 1999' The Boer War' 4 Books p184

4 Ibid p27

5 Gilbert, Adrian. 1950 from the diary of F.M. Crum 'Memoirs of a Rifleman Scout' Frontline Books p22

6 Knight, Ian 1997 'Boer Wars' 1898 -1902 Osprey pub. P24&33

7 Jackson, Tabitha 1999 'The Boer War' 4 Books p78

8 Ibid p82

9 Packenham, Thomas 1988 'The Boer War' Futura p252

10 Ibid p253

11 Beckett, Ian 2003 'The Victorians at War' Hambledon p228

12 Miller, Stephen. 2005 'In Support of the Imperial Mission. Volunteering for the South African War, 1899-1902' The Journal of Military History p69

13 Bennet, Will 'Absent-Minded Beggars' Kindle position 660

14 Winton, Graham. 2018 'Theirs Not To Reason Why'. Helion Press p102

15 Bennet, Will 'Absent-Minded Beggars' Kindle position 1942 (Photo)

16 Ibid pos 1811-2062

17 Pakenham, Thomas 1988 'The Boer War'. Futura p136.

18 Bennet, Will 'Absent-Minded Beggars' Kindle position 1385

[19]   Ibid pos 1438

[20]   Ibid pos 2080 – 2149

[21]   Ibid pos 1351

[22]   Mommsen, Wolfgang. J. 2014 'The International Impact of the Boer War' Routledge p1

[23]   Packenham, Thomas 1988 'The Boer War' Futura pp569-570

[24]   Jackson, Tabitha 1999' The Boer War' 4 Books p184

[25]   http://www.devonheritage.org/Nonplace/DevonReg/Devons2ndBoerWarRollofHonour
        http://www.roll-of-honour.com/Cornwall/TruroCathedralBoerWar.html

[26]   Packenham, Thomas 1988 'The Boer War' Futura p505

[27]   Roberts, Brian. 1991. 'Those Bloody Women' John Murry pp211-212

[28]   Ibid pp208-209

[29]   Jackson, Tabitha 1999' The Boer War' 4 Books p184

[30]   Knight, Ian 1996. 'The Boer War (1)'. Osprey Publications p43

[31]   Tilchin, William. 2001 'The International Impact of the Boer War' Routledge pp107-109

[32]   Bourne, John. 2015 'British Readiness for War' within 'Britain Goes To War' Pen &Sword p31

Chapter Three
It's The Same Old Tommy And The Same Old Jack?

[1]   Godfrey, Fred 1914 Music Hall Song

[2]   Ascoli, David 1981 'The Mons Star.' Harrap p245

[3]   Messenger, Charles 2005 'Call to Arms'. The British Army 1914-18' Cassell p22

[4]   Ibid p20

[5]   Ibid p27

[6]   Ibid p22

[7]   Ibid p23

[8]   Ibid p24

[9]   Ibid p 28

[10]   Pennell, Catriona 2015 'The Shock of War' within 'Britain Goes To War' Pen &Sword p32

[11]   Ibid p23

[12]   Bourne, John 2015 'British Readiness For War' within 'Britain Goes To War' Pen &Sword p23

[13]   Ibid p24

[14]   Beckett, Ian 2007 'Riflemen Form'. Pen &Sword p260

[15]   Westlake, Ray 2020, 'A Guide to the Volunteer Training Corps' Naval & Military Press p7

[15]   Ibid pp30-31

[17]   Ibid pp42-43

[18] Winter, Dennis 1978'Deaths Men' Penguin Books p63

[19] Ibid p63

[20] Mead, Gary 2007 'The Good Soldier'. Biography of Douglas Haig. Atlantic Books p197

[21] Sheffield, G & Bourne, J 2005 'Douglas Haig Diaries and Letters. BCA p83

[22] Holmes, Richard. 2005 'Tommy' Harper Perennial pp91-92

[23] Atkinson, C. 1926. 'The Devonshire Regiment' N&M pp143-195

[24] Wyrall, Edward 1932 'The Duke of Cornwall's Light Infantry 1914 -1919 N&M pp158 -202

Chapter Four
Goodwill to all Men?

[1] Osborne, Mike 2017 'If the Kaiser Comes' Fonthill p24

[2] *Daily Mail,* 11 July 1908, p. 5

[3] Osborne, Mike 2017 'If the Kaiser Comes' Fonthill p24

[4] Ibid p24

[5] MacMillan, Margaret 2014 'The War That Ended Peace' Profile books. pp274 – 281

[6] Ibid p xxiv

[7] Mombauer, Annika 2002 'The Origins of the first World War' Malaysia: Longman p 191

[8] Ponting, Clive 2003 'Thirteen Days.' Pimlico p148

[9] Hattersley, Roy 2004 'The Edwardians'. Abacus p466

[10] Batten, Simon 2018 'Futile Exercise? The British Army's Preparations For War 1902-1914' Helion Press p208

Chapter Five
Semper Fidelis and One for All?

[1] Erskin, N. 2012 'The Role of British newspapers in World War One' British Library P55

[2] Gregory, Adrien 2008 'The Last Great War' Cambridge U. P. p11

[3] Churchill, Winston S. 1938. "X: The Mobilization of the Navy". The World Crisis 1911-1918. Odhams Press p. 186

[4] Bourke, Joanna. 1999. An Intimate History of Killing. Granta Books. p14

[5] Jerrold, Douglas 1923 'The Royal Naval Division'. N&M Press Pxi Introduction

[6] Showalter, Dennis 2016 'Instrument of War.' Osprey Publications p43

[7] Adkin, Mark 2013 'The Western Front Companion.' Arum Press p81

[8] Ibid p81

[9] Ibid p81

[10] Stone, David 2015 'The Kaiser's Army'. Bloomsbury p63

[11] Mead, Gary 2007 'The Good Soldier'. Atlantic Books p198

[12] Messenger, Charles. 2005 'Call to Arms. The British Army 1914-18'. Cassell p131

[13] Ibid p131

[14] Graham, Michael 2014 'Oxford in the Great War'. Pen &Sword p39

[15] Ed: Emmet, Middleton, Page & Warren 2019 'In the Shadow of the Great War'. Surrey 1914-1922. History Press p 22

[16] Hart, Gary 'Fire and Movement' 2015. OUP p107

[17] Bird, Anthony 'Gentlemen We Will Stand And Fight' Crowford Press. P 15

[18] Ibid p15

[19] Hart, Gary 'Fire and Movement' 2015. OUP p125

[20] Ibid p146

[21] Ibid p147

[22] Murland, Jerry 'Retreat and Rearguard' 2014 Pen &Sword. P70

[23] McPhail, H.& Guest P. 'Graves & Sassoon' 2001. Pen &Sword p 31

[24] Jerrold, Douglas. 1923. 'The Royal Naval Division'. Naval & Military Press. pp 44-57

[25] https://www.winchestercollegeatwar.com/RollofHonour

[26] In 1917 Major Quiller-Couch was wounded at the Battle of Third Ypres (Passchendaele) but tragically died during the influenza epidemic while on Occupation duties in Germany. He is recorded on the Fowey memorial.

[27] Osborne, Mike. 2017 If the Kaiser Comes' Fonthill p 159

[28] Spiers, Edward m. 2015 'The National Response to the Outbreak of War 1914' within 'Britain Goes To War' Pen & Sword p55

[29] Gavaghan, Michael 1997 'The Battles of Neuve Chappelle, Aubers Ridge and Festubert 1915 M&L Pubs p8

[30] Barnstaple Gazette. 16th April 1915

[31] Gavaghan, Michael 1997 'The Battles of Neuve Chaplle, Aubers Ridge and Festubert 1915. M&L Pubs pp 93/94

[32] London, Peter 2013 'Cornwall in the Great War' Truran Press p 96
See also Beneath Flanders Fields. The Tunnellers' War 1914-1918 Barton, Doyle and Vandewalle.

[33] Liddle, Peter2016 'Britain and the Widening War 1915-1916 Pen &Sword p4

Chapter Six
The Great Betrayal: Dardanelles and Suvla Bay

[1] Batten, Simon 2018 'Futile Exercise? The British Army's Preparations For War 1902-1914' Helion Press p72

[2] See John Lee 'A Soldiers Life' and John Jones 'Johnny' both studies of Hamilton's life and military career.

3   For example Horace Curtis VC Royal Dublin Fusiliers. 'Cornwall in the First World War '. Truran Press p 89

4   Chambers, Steven 2011, 'Suvla' Pen & Sword p142

Chapter Seven
A Kingdom United?

1   Wade, Stephen 2016 'Leeds in the Great War' Pen & Sword p 219 Kindle edition.

2   Spiers, Edward 2015 'The National Response to the Outbreak of War' within 'Britain Goes To War' pp53-54

3   Turner, William 1998 'Accrington Pals' Wharncliffe Publishing pp 27-29

4   Spiers, Edward 2015 'The National Response to the Outbreak of War' within 'Britain Goes To War 'p 55

5   Graham, Malcolm, 2014 'Oxford in the Great War' Pen & Sword pp37-38

6   Millichope, David 2016 'Britain and the Widening war 1915 -1916' Pen & Sword p169

7   Potter, Alex, 2015 'Torquay in the Great War' Pen & Sword p16

8   Messenger, Charles. 2005, 'Call To Arms' Cassel p105

9   Tait, Derek 2016 'Aberdeen in the Great War' Pen & Sword p22

10   Wadsworth, Jacqueline, 2014, 'Bristol in the Great War' Pen & Sword p17

11   Messenger, Charles. 2005, 'Call To Arms' Cassel p499

12   Atkinson, C.T. 1926 'The Devonshire Regiment 1914 -1918' N&M pp 12-27

13   Turner, Peter 'A Brief History of the 2nd Battalion The Devonshire Regiment 1914 -1918' The Keep. pp1-2

14   Johnson, Tom. 1992 'Orange, Green and Khaki' Gill & Macmillan p12

15   N.J.Erskine. 2012 'The Role of British Newspapers in World War One. British Library p153

16   McPhail, Helen. 2001 'The Long Silence. Civilian Life under the German occupation of France 1914 -1918' I.B.Tauris Publishers.

Appendices
One

1   Johnstone, Tom. 1992 'Orange, Green and Khaki. Gill and Macmillan Ltd. pp419-420

2   Dunn, Steve R,2018, 'Bayly's War'. Seaforth Publishing pp 170 -173

3   Ibid pp 69-73

4   Ibid pp 72- 73

5   London, Peter, 2013 'Cornwall in the First World War'. Truran Pub. p97

6   Nash, N.S. 2010 'Chitral Charlie'. Pen & Sword p26

7   Ibid p263

8   Ibid p 242

Two

1   Wyrall, Evereard 1927 (1919) 'The History of the Somerset Light Infantry (Prince Albert's) 1914 – 1919'. Making History p267

2   Ibid pp 271 -272

3   Cite : Gott Mit Uns (http://ww1centenary.oucs.ox.ac.uk/?p=1638) by Everett Sharp

4   Simkins, Jukes & Hickey2003.' The First World War' Osprey Publications p 129

5   Snelling, Stephen 2002. 'The Naval VCs'. Sutton Publishing p121

6   Newbolt, H. 2009 (1931). Naval Operations.

7   See Kendall. Paul 2009. 'The Zeebrugge Raid' The History Press for an excellent account of the planning and events *surrounding* Operation ZO

8   Ibid p 318-323

9   Janes Fighting Ships of World War 1. 1990 (1st 1919) p80

10   Wright, Damien. 2017. 'Churchill's Secret War With Lenin'. Helion Press pp362 -363

11   Ibid pp364 -369

12   Tooze, Adam 2015. 'The Deluge. The remaking of Global Order.' Penguin p415

13   Wright, Damian. 2017. 'Churchill's Secret War With Lenin'. Helion Press p371

14   Three VCs were awarded overall. Commander Agar for the first attack in June, Lt. Steele and also Lt. Claude Dobson, Commander of CMB 31 for the second in August.

15   Watts, Anthony.1999 'The Royal Navy'. Naval Institute Press pp 124-125.

16   Konstam, Angus. 'Warships In The Baltic Campaign 1918 -20'. Osprey Publications p18 Kindle edition.

Three

1   For an in depth history see Hogg, Ian. The Illustrated History of Firearms, 1983. Newnes Books pgs24 -47 Also, for the ease of concealment see Pakenham, Thomas. The Boer War. 1988. Macdonald and Co. p137

2   Hogg, Ian. The Illustrated History of Firearms, 1983. Newnes Books pgs310-311

3   Orange Green and Khaki.1992. Johnstone, Tom. Gilland & Macmillan p45 - 47.

4   https://www.hi.uni-stuttgart.de/wgt/ww-one/Start/Bleed_White/ Technology_and_Science/ww1_ger_08_05.html